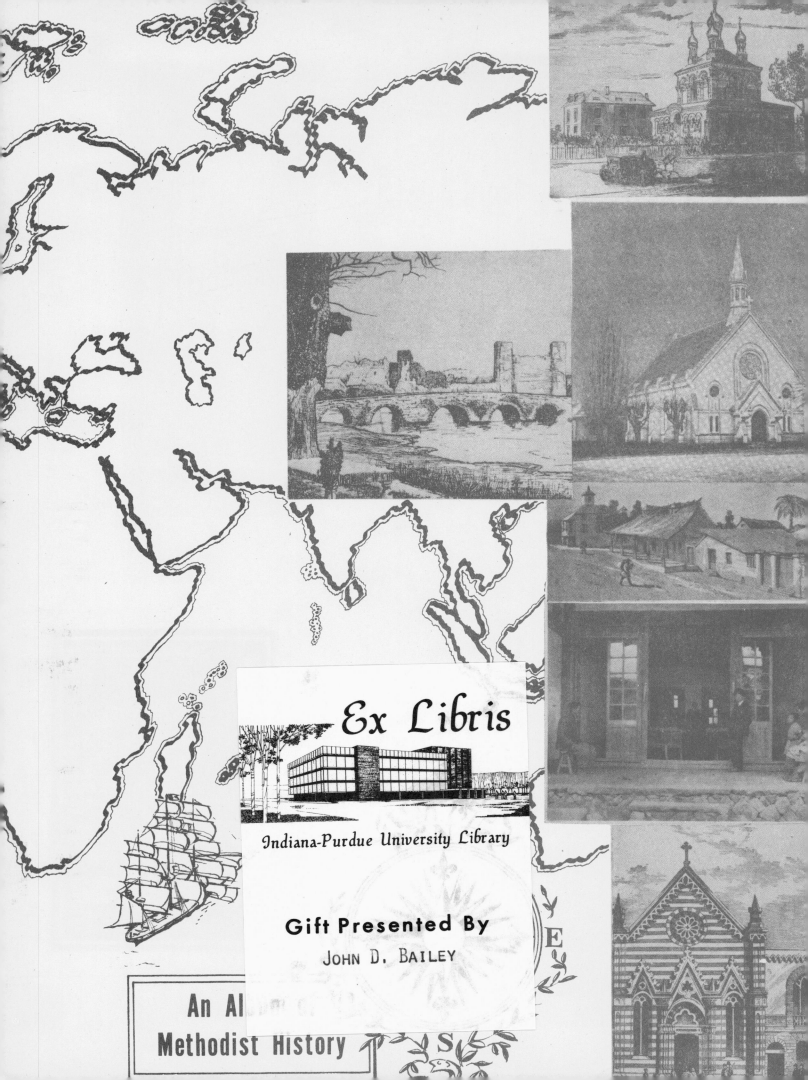

An Al...
Methodist History

An Album of
Methodist History

AN ALBUM OF **METHODIST** HISTORY

by ELMER T. CLARK

New York   Nashville

ABINGDON-COKESBURY PRESS

AN ALBUM OF METHODIST HISTORY

COPYRIGHT MCMLII
BY PIERCE AND SMITH

Library of Congress Catalog Card Number: 52-5733

SET UP, PRINTED, AND BOUND BY THE
PARTHENON PRESS, AT NASHVILLE,
TENNESSEE, UNITED STATES OF AMERICA

Preface

THE Methodist Movement has spread to nearly every nation under the sun and is now represented by forty independent Methodist bodies in seventy-five countries. The whole communion has a membership of more than sixteen million souls, and a constituency of eighty or ninety million; it is therefore probably the greatest free church the world has ever seen.

If one should attempt to portray in pictures the past history and present status of ecumenical Methodism, "even the world itself could not contain the books that should be written." Certainly no task so ambitious is here undertaken. My purpose has been far more modest. It has been necessary to confine the materials almost exclusively to Methodist beginnings and to illustrate the outstanding events only.

I experience difficulty in acknowledging my indebtedness to all the sources on which I have drawn. My own collection of prints has been gathered from many countries over a period of many years, and the sources from which they were derived cannot always be determined. I have had access to the tens of thousands of photographs and pictures of various kinds and of course to the numerous illustrated histories that have been published in America and elsewhere. Many individuals and institutions have been most co-operative in supplying material. It will, of course, be noted that most of the pictures in this book are neither new nor unknown; the Methodist "Classics" have been liberally used and numerous illustrations have been taken from old books which were widely circulated in the past.

When possible, there has been acknowledgment of sources in connection with the pictures. Mention should be made of the following volumes which have been useful and from the pages of which certain pictures have been taken: Hurst: *The History of Methodism*, 7 vols.; Buckley: *History of Methodism*, 2 vols.; Daniels: *The Illustrated History of Methodism*; Stevens: *History of Methodism*, 3 vols.; Scudder: *American Methodism*; Hyde: *The Story of Methodism*; Barker: *History of Ohio Methodism*; Simpson: *Cyclopaedia of Methodism*; Lee, Luccock, and Dixon: *The Illustrated History of Methodism*; *Wesley and His Successors*; Billingsley: *Life of Whitefield*; Clark: *The Wesley Memorial Volume*; Finney: *Life and Labors of Enoch Mather Marvin*; Jones: *Christ In the Camp*; Drewry: *The Story of a Church*; Dunford: *History of Central Methodist Church*. Dr. J. Manning Potts and Dr. Alpheus W. Potts supplied some pictures of Virginia churches. Special gratitude is expressed to the noted British artist, Frank O. Salisbury, for the use of his two modern portraits of John Wesley.

The Reverend Frank Baker, British Secretary of the International Methodist Historical Society and Executive Secretary of the Wesley Historical Society, has been extraordinarily kind and co-operative; not only did he furnish several photographs, but with great care and expert historical scholarship he checked and revised the titles of all the pictures pertaining to Great Britain. For the American section a similarly expert and painstaking service was rendered by Dr. Jacob S. Payton, president of the Association of Methodist Historical Societies of the Northeastern Jurisdiction of The Methodist Church, U.S.A. Miss Dorothy Magee kindly permitted the use of the pictures of the Bishops of The Methodist Church which she had gathered. To these good friends I acknowledge a heavy debt and express deep gratitude.

This volume has been prepared under the sponsorship of the World Methodist Council, its affiliate, the International Methodist Historical Society, and the Association of Methodist Historical Societies in the United States of America.

ELMER T. CLARK

Contents

SECTION 1—BRITISH METHODISM

SECTION 2—AMERICAN METHODISM

SECTION 1

British Methodism

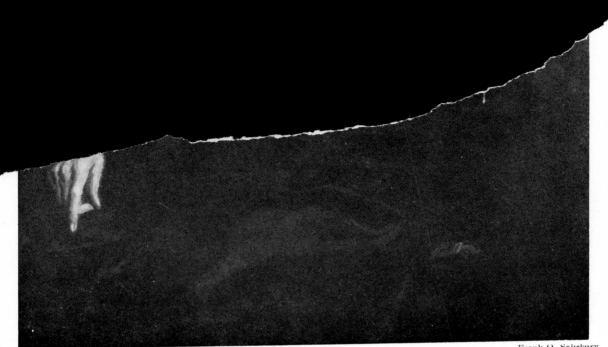

JOHN WESLEY, FOUNDER OF METHODISM

In those clear, piercing eyes behold
The very soul that over England flamed!

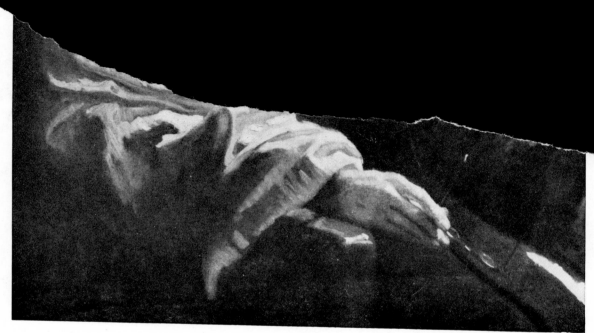

JOHN WESLEY

Frank O. Salisbury

Methodism is the "lengthened shadow" of John Wesley, whose life covered almost the whole of the eighteenth century. He was born at Epworth on June 17, 1703, and died in London on March 2, 1791.

Social Conditions in Eighteenth-Century England

METHODISM arose as a revolt against nearly every aspect of English life, including religion and the Church. British historians have described the low state of morals, culture, and human relations, and the artist Hogarth lashed out in numerous paintings which give a terrible picture of English society.

Hogarth

"INDUSTRY AND IDLENESS"

One of a series, this picture shows the climax of idleness as a condemned man and his coffin are taken to the place of execution. Silas Todd, a Methodist preacher, reads the Scriptures to the culprit. Two hundred offenses were punishable by death, and a popular pastime was that of watching public hangings and whippings.

15

Hogarth

"THE SLEEPING CONGREGATION"

Deism existed in the Church, and sermons were preached on "Be not righteous over much!" Although Christian piety prevailed in many places, religion shared in the general degradation of the times and was publicly ridiculed. Clergymen confined in prisons were allowed to marry couples, and one such performed 6,000 of these "ruinous marriages" in one year. Even the agnostic Voltaire was shocked at the morals of the clergy, and Montesquieu declared, "There is no religion in England. . . . If one speaks of religion, everybody begins to laugh. . . . In France I am thought to have too little religion, but in England to have too much."

"CREDULITY, SUPERSTITION, AND FANATICISM"

The parson dangles an imp and a witch, a Turk peers
through the window on a cauldron of confusion, and John
Wesley's volumes of sermons lie on the floor.

"BEER STREET"

Every sixth house in London was a saloon, and England
qualified as the most drunken nation in the world.

Hogarth

"GIN LANE"

"Drunk for a penny; dead drunk for twopence; clean straw for nothing," was a common sign in London. Liquor was deliberately made cheap and its use encouraged. In 1740 there were twice as many burials as baptisms, and in 1750 the death rate was one in twenty.

The Wesley Ancestry

THE Wesley family may have sprung from the West Meadow seat of a Wessex family in early Norman times. It variously appears as Wesley, Westley, Westleigh, and Wellesley. In the time of Queen Elizabeth, Sir Herbert Westley, of Westleigh, married Elizabeth de Wellesley of Dangan, in Ireland, and thus united with another name destined to become famous in English history. Westley of Dangan later desired to adopt Charles Wesley and did actually send the young man to Westminster School. When Charles Wesley declined adoption, "fearing lest worldly prosperity and its consequences might lead away his heart from due attention to his eternal interests," the Irish relative adopted Richard Colley of Dublin, who became the first Earl of Mornington and the grandfather of the Marquis Wellesley and the Duke of Wellington.

Remains of the jail at Poole where John Westley of Whitchurch was imprisoned

from Hurst

The Wesley home in Ireland, Trim on the Boyne, was represented in Parliament (1790-95) by Arthur Wellesley, later Duke of Wellington. Dangan Castle is four miles distant.

Dorchester, where Samuel Wesley first went to school

19

John Wesley (or Westley) of Whitchurch (1636-78),
the grandfather of John Wesley, was an M.A. of Oxford
and a clergyman of the Church of England, approved by
Cromwell's "triers" or ecclesiastical committee. On the
overthrow of Cromwell's Protectorate he was jailed four
times and expelled from his Winterborn Whitchurch parish
for refusing to use the *Book of Common Prayer*. His
father, Reverend Bartholomew Wesley (or Westley), was
also ejected from his parish under the Act of Uniformity
because of his sympathy with the Puritans.

Hall of Exeter College, Oxford, where John Wesley's father was educated

Samuel Wesley (1662-1735), the father of the Founder of Methodism, was born four months after his father and grandfather, with two thousand other clergymen, were ejected from their parishes by the Act of Uniformity, which demanded "unfeigned assent and consent" to the *Book of Common Prayer*. But he broke the family tradition by becoming a Tory in politics and a High-churchman. He was a prolific writer and the author of the well-known hymn, "Behold the Saviour of Mankind."

Samuel Wesley at nineteen

The Mother of Methodism

SUSANNA WESLEY (1669-1742), the mother of Methodism, was one of the great women of history. Adam Clarke said that he had "never seen, heard, or read of her equal." She was the mother of nineteen children, ten of whom lived to maturity; some died in infancy, and only thirteen have been identified by name.

Susanna Wesley

Susanna Wesley

Epworth

I N 1693 Samuel Wesley published a "Life of Christ" in verse and dedicated it to Queen Anne. In return he was made rector of Epworth in Lincolnshire, which he served for thirty-nine years until his death. The life of the Wesley family was closely associated with Epworth, and its name has entered into the Methodist vocabulary.

The Baptismal Font at Epworth Church where John Wesley was baptized

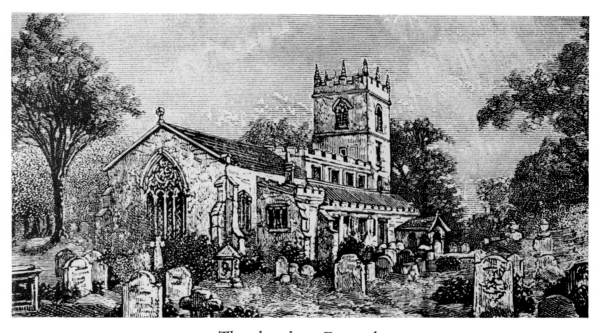

The church at Epworth

Susanna Wesley and the Epworth parishioners

Samuel Wesley was a member of the Convocation of the Church of England and was in London for extended periods. During these absences Mrs. Wesley conducted devotions at home, first for the children and later for the neighbors also. Samuel wrote in protest, and she replied that she would continue to exhort unless he sent her a "positive command" to desist. The services continued!

Susanna Wesley preaching in Epworth Rectory

Spital Yard, London, birthplace of Susanna Wesley

St. Giles's, Cripplegate, where Dr. Samuel Annesley, father of John Wesley's mother, was vicar, 1658-62

Dr. Samuel Annesley (1620-96), father of Susanna Wesley, was a nephew of the Earl of Anglesea and a man of deep learning and piety. He was a clergyman and was ejected from his parish under the Act of Uniformity. Thus both the grandfathers of John and Charles Wesley were persecuted under that law. Annesley later became one of the leading nonconformist ministers of England.

Samuel Wesley's tomb at Epworth, on which John Wesley preached when he was refused the use of the pulpit

The Rectory

SAMUEL and Susanna Wesley moved into Epworth Rectory in 1696, and here they reared their numerous children, though some were born at South Ormsby, and the eldest, Samuel, was born in London. Fire destroyed the first rectory at midnight on February 9, 1709. Young John Wesley, trapped by the flames, was saved by a "human ladder," and he afterward referred to himself as "a brand plucked out of the burning."

Epworth Rectory
in 1823

The new rectory built after the fire

Rescue of John Wesley from the fire

Lincoln Castle, where Samuel Wesley was imprisoned for six months in 1705 for debt, probably at the instigation of parishioners who were displeased by his political sentiments

Old Jeffrey's room. The new Epworth Rectory was "haunted" by a ghost. The Wesleys seemingly believed in the Polter-geist and named him "Old Jeffrey."

"*I thank you, I will think of it.*"

Susanna Wesley's children learned their letters in one day on their fifth birthday. Two who took a day and a half she "then thought very dull."

Scenes at Charterhouse School. John Wesley entered the famous Charterhouse School in London when he was about eleven years old. He remained there for six years.

John Wesley at Thirteen Years of Age. This picture was published in the *Standard Letters of John Wesley*, but its authenticity seems to be in question.

28

John Wesley at Charterhouse

Charterhouse School, a former Carthusian monastery which was suppressed by Henry VIII, was made into a boys' school by Thomas Sutton in 1611. Many famous men were trained here, among them being Addison, Steele, and Blackstone. Writing in later years, Wesley indicated that he did not grow in grace at the Charterhouse: "What I now hoped to be saved by was (1) not being as bad as other people; (2) having still a kindness for religion; and (3) reading the Bible, going to Church, and saying my prayers."

JOHN WESLEY entered Christ Church College at Oxford in 1720, remaining for five years. Though he later wrote that at Oxford he "had not so much as a notion of inward holiness" and "cannot well tell what I hoped to be saved by," he became deeply interested in religion in 1725 and resolved to become a clergyman.

In 1726 he was elected a Fellow of Lincoln College, a distinction which caused his father to exclaim, "What will be my own fate God only knows. . . . Whatever I am, my Jack is Fellow of Lincoln." The office carried a stipend about sixty pounds a year, and Wesley retained it until 1751.

Christ Church College at Oxford

Wesley's Rooms at Lincoln College, Oxford

"Rules of Holy Living" in John Wesley's shorthand

> *Ego Iohannes Wesley Collegii Lincolniensis in Academia Oxoniensi Socius, quicquid mihi juris est in prædictâ Societate, ejusdem Rectori & Sociis sponte ac liberè resigno: Illis universis et singulis perpetuam pacem ac omnimodam in Christo felicitatem exoptans.*
>
> *Londini:*   *Iohannes Wesley.*
> *Kalendis Iunii:*
> *Anno Salutis, Millesimo, Septingentesimo, Quinquagesimo Primo*

Wesley's Resignation of his Oxford Fellowship, June 1, 1751.
He was a Fellow of Oxford for twenty-six years.

Wroot Church. In 1727 Wesley became his father's curate at Wroot, a neighboring parish, though against his own desires. He served until 1729, when he was recalled to Oxford, where he lectured until 1735. Of his pastoral experience Wesley later wrote: "I drew no crowds; I alarmed no consciences; I preached much but saw no fruit of my labor."

Reverend John Potter, Bishop of Oxford, ordained John Wesley as deacon in 1725 and as presbyter in 1728.

Wroot Rectory

South Leigh Church near Oxford, where John Wesley preached his first sermon

The Holy Club At Oxford

IN 1729, under the leadership of Charles Wesley, a group was organized at Oxford for Christian living and service, and when John Wesley returned from Wroot he became its leader. Because of their systematic routine in devotions and good works the members in derision were called Bible Bigots, Bible Moths, the Holy Club, the Godly Club, and Methodists. The last name, which had been applied to other religious enthusiasts, stuck to and was appropriated by the group, and Wesley's later followers became "The People Called Methodists." The known members of the Holy Club were John and Charles Wesley, George Whitefield, Thomas Broughton, James Hervey, Robert Kirkham, Benjamin Ingham, William Morgan, John Gambold, John Clayton, Charles Kinchin, Christopher Atkinson, Charles Morgan, William Smith, Matthew Salmon, William Clapham, Richard Hutchins, John Whitelamb, Westley Hall, and John Boyce.

The Holy Club

Bocardo Prison, Oxford, in which the members of the Holy Club did works of mercy

—from Hurst

JOHN CLAYTON

THOMAS BROUGHTON

JAMES HERVEY

BENJAMIN INGHAM

JOHN GAMBOLD

Some Members of the Holy Club

—from Hurst

"I AM A MAN OF ONE BOOK"—C. S. Reinhart

In order to save money the Wesley brothers sometimes walked from Oxford to Epworth, reading as they went. They walked in Indian file, so that the one behind could be less alert than the one in front.

The Mission to Georgia

ON October 14, 1735, both John and Charles Wesley sailed on the ship "Simmonds" for General James Oglethorpe's colony in Georgia, Charles as the General's secretary and John as chaplain and missionary. With them sailed Benjamin Ingham of the Holy Club and Charles Delamotte. John Wesley thus stated his reason for the journey: "My chief motive is the hope of saving my own soul. I hope to learn the true sense of the gospel of Christ by preaching it to the heathen."

John Wesley in a Moravian meeting on shipboard

General James Oglethorpe, (1696-1785)

Wesley and the Moravians in the storm. On board the "Simmonds" were twenty-six Moravians from Count Zinzendorf's Moravian community at Herrnhut in Germany. John Wesley was deeply impressed with their calm behavior in a storm. "Weren't you afraid?" he asked. "I thank God, no," replied their leader, "our women and children are not afraid to die." This was the beginning of an association with Moravians that profoundly influenced Wesley's religious life.

The landing of the "Simmonds" at Savannah. The Wesleys landed at Savannah, a town of forty houses, on February 5, 1736. John Wesley consulted August Spangenberg, the Moravian pastor, about his work. "Do you know Jesus Christ?" inquired the Moravian. "I know He is the Saviour of the world," replied Wesley. "But do you know He has saved you?" persisted Spangenberg. "I do," was the reply, but in his *Journal* Wesley wrote, "I fear they were vain words."

August Gottlieb Spangenberg (1704-1792), Moravian pastor in Georgia

David Nitschmann, Moravian bishop, who sailed with Wesley to Savannah

COLLECTION

OF

PSALMS

AND

HYMNS.

CHARLES-TOWN,
Printed by Lewis Timothy. 1737.

Title page of Wesley's hymnbook published at Charleston in 1737. John Wesley gathered some of the colonists and their children on Sunday afternoon for a service, and this is the basis of a disputed claim that he founded the world's first Sunday school. More important is the fact that he published at Charleston the first hymnal ever issued in America and the first of many published by the Wesleys and their followers. Only two copies are now known to exist.

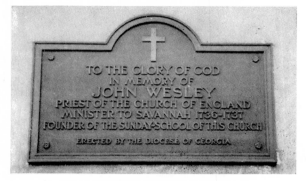

Wesley Tablet on Christ Church (Episcopal) at Savannah

Wesley Tablet on the site of the old Court House at Savannah

THE FIRST
CHURCH SCHOOL

"To the glory of God, in memory of John Wesley, priest of the Church of England, Minister to Savannah, 1736-1737. Founder of the Sunday School of the Church. Erected by the Diocese of Georgia."

Commemorative plaque at Savannah

Tomo Chachi, chief of the Indians in Georgia

—from an old print

John Wesley conversing with the Indians. John Wesley desired to do missionary work among the Indians, and he had a long conference with their chief, Tomo Chachi. "They are as little children," he wrote, "humble, willing to learn, and do the will of God." He soon changed his mind about them, however, and denounced them as pagans and criminals, for he was unable to make any headway in his efforts to evangelize them. He concentrated on his work as the spiritual overseer of the white colonists.

Preaching to the Indians in Georgia

The Wesley Oak on St. Simon's Island, Georgia, under which John Wesley is said to have preached

Ruins of the Citadel, Fort Frederica, on St. Simon's Island, Georgia, built by Oglethorpe in 1736

JOHN WESLEY began the writing of his famous *Journal* with his mission to Georgia, continuing it until near the end of his life. He had previously (April, 1725) started a diary, which he also continued. Much of the diary was in a form of shorthand and a cipher which Wesley invented. The *Journals*, edited by the Rev. Nehemiah Curnock in ten large volumes, are among the world's greatest and most important religious literature.

A N

EXTRACT

O F T H E

Rev. Mr. JOHN WESLEY'S

JOURNAL

From his Embarking for GEORGIA

To his Return to LONDON.

What shall we say then?——That Israel which follow'd after the Law of Righteousness, hath not attained to the Law of Righteousness.—— Wherefore? Because they sought it not by Faith, but as it were by the Works of the Law. Rom. ix. 30, 31.

BRISTOL:

Printed by S. and F. FARLEY.

And sold at the New School-Houfe in the Horfe-Fair: and by the Bookfellers in Town and Country.

Title page of the first edition of John Wesley's *Journal*

The PREFACE.

1. IT was in Purfuance of an **Advice** given by Bp. *Taylor*, in his *Rules for Holy Living and Dying*, that about fifteen Years ago, I began to take a more exact Account than I had done before, of the manner wherein I fpent my **Time**, writing down how I had employed **every** Hour. This I continued to de, wherever I was, till the Time of my leaving *England*. The Variety of Scenes which I then paft thro', induced me to tranfcribe from time to time, the more material Parts of my Diary, adding here and there fuch little Reflections as occurr'd to my Mind. Of this Journal thus occafionally compiled, the following is a fhort Extract: It not being my Defign to relate all thofe Particulars, which I wrote for my own Ufe only; and which would anfwer no valuable End to others, however important they were to me.

2. Indeed I had no Defign or Defire to trouble the World with any of my little Affairs: As can't but appear to every impartial Mind, from my having been fo long *as one that heareth not*, notwithftanding the loud and frequent Calls I have had, to anfwer for myfelf. Neither fhou'd I
have

Preface to the first edition of John Wesley's *Journal*

Title pages of some of Wesley's publications. John Wesley wrote or edited more than three hundred books and pamphlets, which he published in cheap editions and scattered far and wide. Most famous were his *Journal, Sermons,* and *Notes on the New Testament.* His *Christian Library* contained extracts from many works and was in fifty volumes. *Primitive Physick* was a collection of curious prescriptions for numerous diseases, which ran through nearly two dozen editions.

A
Chriſtian Library.

CONSISTING OF

EXTRACTS from and ABRIDGMENTS of

THE

CHOICEST PIECES

OF

Practical Divinity,

Which have been publiſh'd in the

ENGLISH TONGUE

In FIFTY VOLUMES.

By JOHN WESLEY, M.A.

FELLOW of Lincoln-College, OXFORD.

VOL. I.

BRISTOL:

Printed by FELIX FARLEY.

M.DCC.XLIX.

—from the Clark collection of first editions

John Wesley's Christian library

Wesley Monumental Methodist Church at Savannah, Georgia

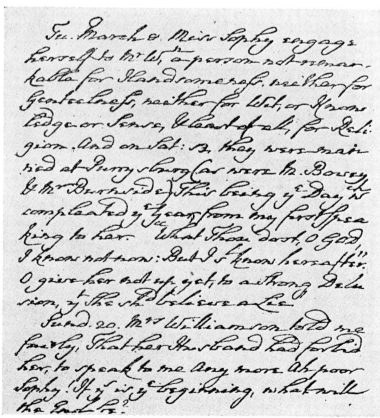

—from Hurst

In his *Journal* written at Savannah, Wesley refers to Miss Sophy Hopkey, with whom he had a love affair which led to his departure from Georgia. Wesley was indicted for excluding her from the Holy Communion after she married another man.

Aldersgate

THE Wesleyan Revival issued directly from the notable religious experiences of John and Charles Wesley at Whitsuntide in 1738. To the end of his life John Wesley traced the genesis of his experience, doctrines, and power back to 1738. Wesley's awakening involved several steps:

1. Wesley returned from Georgia in deep spiritual dejection. In his writings he reproached himself over and over again as a sinner, saying that he was "carnal, sold under sin," in a "vile, abject state of bondage to sin," "altogether corrupt and abominable," and "a child of wrath and an heir of hell."

2. On February 7, 1738, he met a Moravian, Peter Böhler, who told him that salvation was by faith alone. Wesley had sought salvation by "works" also.

3. Wesley demanded proof of the doctrine from scripture and living witnesses. These were supplied, and Wesley wrote, "I was now clearly convinced of unbelief."

4. Wesley's first impulse was to cease preaching. "How can you preach to others who have no faith yourself?" he wrote. The Moravian said, "Preach faith till you have it; then because you have it, you *will* preach faith."

5. On March 6, 1738, John Wesley began preaching salvation by faith in Christ alone. Great success attended his ministry, and more than a quarter of a century later he wrote, "Then God began to work by my ministry, as he had never done before."

6. On April 21 Peter Böhler told Wesley that saving faith could be secured by an instantaneous work of grace. Wesley "could not comprehend what he spoke of," but again the Moravian proved it by scripture and living witnesses. "Here ended my dispute," wrote Wesley. "I could only cry out, 'Lord, help thou my unbelief!' "

7. Charles Wesley at first strongly opposed these doctrines but on May 3 he had a conference with Peter Böhler and accepted them. A few days later he was sick in the home of one Mr. Bray, "a poor mechanic, who knows nothing but Christ," in Little Britain, near Aldersgate Street, London. Here William Holland read Luther's remarks on the second chapter of Galatians, and the words, "He loved me and gave himself for me," went to Charles Wesley's heart. On May 21 he "found a deeper rest for his soul," and on May 23, to use his own words, "I waked under the protection of Christ and gave myself up, soul and body, to Him." He at once wrote a hymn, probably, "Where shall my wondering soul begin?"

8. In a religious meeting in Aldersgate Street, at 8:45 P.M., May 24, 1738, while one was reading Luther's preface to Romans and describing salvation by faith, John Wesley felt his heart "strangely warmed." This was the famous Aldersgate Awakening. Wesley felt an assurance of salvation; he began to pray for his enemies, and he testified to those present that he had received the experience.

9. John Wesley went "with a troop of friends" to Charles Wesley's bedside in the Bray home. "I believe!" cried John. Then the company sang the hymn which Charles had written the day before. Called the "Birth Song of Methodism," it remains in the hymnbook of the British church and is greatly treasured, although it no longer appears in the American hymnal.

Wesley's experience at Aldersgate. "In the evening I went very unwillingly to a society in Aldersgate Street, where one was reading Luther's preface to the Epistle to the Romans. About a quarter before nine, while he was describing the change which God works in the heart through faith in Christ, I felt my heart strangely warmed. I felt I did trust in Christ, Christ alone for salvation: and an assurance was given me, that he had taken away *my* sins, even *mine*, and saved *me* from the law of sin and death.

"I began to pray with all my might for those who had in a more especial manner despitefully used me and persecuted me. I then testified openly to all there what I now first felt in my heart."

—John Wesley's *Journal*, May 24, 1738

The "Birth Song" of the Methodist Revival written by Charles Wesley

Where shall my wondering soul begin?
  How shall I all to heaven aspire?
A slave redeemed from death and sin,
  A brand plucked from eternal fire,
How shall I equal triumphs raise,
Or sing my great Deliverer's praise?

O how shall I the goodness tell,
  Father, which Thou to me hast showed?
That I, a child of wrath and hell,
  I should be called a child of God,
Should know, should feel my sins forgiven,
Blest with this antepast of heaven?

And shall I slight my Father's love?
  Or basely fear His gifts to own?
Unmindful of his favors prove?
  Shall I, the hallowed cross to shun,
Refuse His righteousness to impart,
By hiding it within my heart?

Outcasts of men, to you I call,
  Harlots, and publicans and thieves!
He spreads His arms to embrace you all;
  Sinners alone His grace receives:
No need of Him the righteous have;
He came the lost to seek and save.

Come, O my guilty brethren, come,
  Groaning beneath your load of sin!
His bleeding heart shall make you room,
  His open side shall take you in;
He calls you now, invites you home:
Come, O my guilty brethren, come!

Singing the "Birth Song" of the Methodist Revival,
at the bedside of Charles Wesley in Bray's House
in Little Britain, London, May 24, 1738

—from Hurst

Little Britain, London, in which was located the home of Mr. Bray, where Charles Wesley was converted

The Aldersgate window in City Road Chapel, London

The Bray House, where Charles Wesley's awakening occurred, 1738

Peter Böhler (1712-75)

Wesley in Germany

FOLLOWING his experience at Aldersgate, Wesley set out for Germany with his old friend and associate, Benjamin Ingham, and six other companions to visit the Moravians at Herrnhut ("the watch of the Lord"), where they had settled under the protection of the Saxon Count Zinzendorf. Wesley believed that the opportunity of "conversing with those holy men who were themselves living witnesses of the full power of faith" would help to solidify his own new-found faith. His belief was amply justified, even though he could never condone the high position of authority accorded Count Zinzendorf.

Count Zinzendorf

John Wesley and Count Zinzendorf

Field Preaching

WHEN John Wesley, prior to his Aldersgate experience, began preaching the doctrines of justification by faith alone, instantaneous conversion, and the witness of the Spirit, one by one the churches were closed against him. Anglicanism sought to silence him, but in reality it made the Methodist revival possible, for it eventually forced Wesley to the fields, where the multitudes could be reached, and set the evangelical message blazing all over England.

"Sir, you must preach here no more."

George Whitefield (1714-70). A member of the Oxford "Holy Club" and thus a charter member of the Methodist group, Whitefield was the orator of the movement and one of the greatest preachers of all time. He began the practice of outdoor preaching. He visited America several times, founded the Orphan House at Savannah, was one of the founders of the University of Pennsylvania, and electrified the colonies by his evangelistic preaching. He died in America, on September 30, 1770, and was buried in the Presbyterian Church at Newburyport, Massachusetts. He believed in the Calvinistic doctrine of predestination and broke with Wesley on that subject, though their affection for each other endured.

George Whitefield at 24

—from Billingsley

George Whitefield as a "Pot Boy." Whitefield was born at the Bell Inn at Gloucester and in boyhood was "a professed and common carrier" in the tavern. He attended Oxford as a "servitor."

Whitefield mobbed

—from Billingsley

Whitefield preaching at a horse race

—from Billingsley

—from Hurst

Kennington Common in London, a scene of Whitefield's
early field preaching

—from Billingsley

Field preaching. Whitefield began field preaching at Kingswood, near Bristol, to the
miners, who were called the "beasts of men." Leaving for Georgia, Whitefield urged
John Wesley to take over the work, but the whole idea was repugnant to the correct
and proper presbyter of the Church of England, who declared that he "should have
thought the saving of souls almost a sin," if it had not been done in a church. But the
scene he witnessed persuaded him, and on April 2, 1739, he "submitted to be more
vile," to use his own words, and preached in the open air from the text, "The spirit
of the Lord is upon me, because he hath anointed me to preach the gospel to the poor."

Whitefield preaching at Moorfields in London

Wesley preaching at Gwennap Pit. Wesley preached in the natural amphitheatre at Gwennap, in Cornwall, to thousands. One one occasion, when he was seventy years of age, there were 30,000 people, and his voice could be heard clearly by all. He wrote: "I think this is one of the most magnificent spectacles which is to be seen on this side heaven, and no music is to be heard upon earth comparable to the sound of many thousand voices when they are all harmoniously joined together singing praises to God and the Lamb."

John Wesley preaching on his father's tomb at Epworth
after having been barred from the church

John Wesley preaching on his father's tomb

John Wesley preaching on his father's tomb. On June 6, 1742, Wesley returned to Epworth, where the curate refused to allow him to participate in the service and even preached against him. That afternoon Wesley took his stand upon the flat top of his father's tomb in the churchyard and preached to "such a congregation as I believe Epworth never saw before." His text was, "The kingdom of God is not meat and drink; but righteousness, and peace, and joy in the Holy Ghost." This was a famous episode, and the scene is on Wesley's tablet in Westminster Abbey.

"JOHN WESLEY PREACHING FROM
A MARKET CROSS"

—William Hatherell

John Wesley preaching at Bolton Cross. John Wesley visited Scotland twenty times, Ireland twenty-one times, Wales twenty-four times. In 1764, during a typical but not especially unusual period of 128 days, he toured the length of England and Scotland and back, preached three hundred times in 122 towns, met all the societies, and had but one day of rest.

John Wesley crossing a stream. Now began the itineracy of John Wesley. He became "the soul that over England flamed." For fifty years he rode throughout the British Isles, along every road in England, Scotland, Wales, and Ireland, preaching in every conceivable place, facing daily perils to life and limb, displaying amazing fortitude. Reading and writing as he rode along, he traveled a quarter of a million miles and preached 42,000 times.

John Wesley preaching in Newgate Prison, London

John Wesley assailed by a mob

Persecution

WESLEY was often assaulted and persecuted, and frequently the clergy and magistrates instigated and participated in the attacks. In 1741 he was stoned in London, and two years later there was a riot at Wednesbury. Struck in the face with a missile, he wiped away the blood and continued preaching, but carried the scar to his grave. On one occasion he was taken from a mob by a bully who carried him across a river. Wesley wrote: "It came into my mind that if they should throw me into the river, it would spoil the papers that were in my pocket."

—from an old print

Wesley passing through a ferocious mob

Wesley in a riot in Wednesbury

"MOBBING THE PREACHER"

—from Hurst

At Plymouth a mob which included soldiers set upon Wesley. He walked quietly down and took the captain by the hand. "Sir, no man shall touch you," said the mob leader. "Gentlemen, stand off. Get back. I will knock the first man down that touches him." "We walked on in great peace and parted in much love," said Wesley. "I stayed in the street nearly half an hour after he was gone, talking with the people, who now forgot their anger."

—from Hurst

"THE PREACHER'S CHAMPION"—H. S. Hubbell

"Parson" Butler leading an attack on the Methodist Chapel at Cork, in Ireland. There were assaults upon Wesley and the Methodists in Ireland, where drums, bells, and horns were used to drown out their services, and cattle were turned into their open-air meetings. "It was my rule," wrote Wesley, "confirmed by long experience, always to look a mob in the face."

—from an old print

An Irish Methodist preacher meeting a persecutor

66

Arresting a Methodist

—from Hurst

Scenes of the martyrdom of William Seward: *upper left*, grave of William Seward; *right*, Old Chapel at Hay; *lower*, scene of Seward's martyrdom. The first Methodist martyr was William Seward, who accompanied George Whitefield on one of the latter's trips to America. Blinded by stones at Caerleon, he was killed by a ruffian while preaching at the village of Hay on October 22, 1741. Before dying he prayed for his murderer and begged that no attempt should be made to punish him.

The First Methodist Chapel

WESLEY in 1739 built a small building at Bristol known after remodeling as the New Room. The New Room still stands, the oldest Methodist shrine in the world. It is known as John Wesley's Chapel, Broadmead, Bristol.

The Old Room in the Horsefair, Bristol, the first Methodist meetinghouse

The New Room in the Horsefair, Bristol, after the building was remodeled and enlarged. It was variously called "Schoolroom," "New School," "New Room."

John Wesley laying the cornerstone of the first Methodist chapel in the Horsefair, Bristol, May 12, 1739

Stable for the preachers' horses at the New Room, Bristol

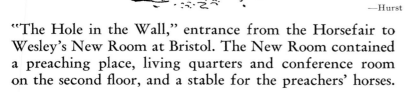

—Hurst

"The Hole in the Wall," entrance from the Horsefair to Wesley's New Room at Bristol. The New Room contained a preaching place, living quarters and conference room on the second floor, and a stable for the preachers' horses.

The John Wesley Statue
at Bristol

Charles Wesley's
Home in Bristol

The Class Meeting

EARLY Methodism had a threefold plan of organization: (1) the Society, consisting of all members who met and worshiped together; (2) the Class, composed of around a dozen Society members, under a Class Leader, which received financial contributions and had weekly meetings for testimony, religious experience, and discipline; (3) the Band, smaller groups of persons of the same sex and marital status formed for similar purposes. The Band disappeared, but the Class Meeting continued in all branches of Methodism until near the twentieth century and still continues in many places. The first Class Meeting was at Bristol in 1742. Afterwards, admission was by ticket, the quarterly ticket being proof of good standing in the Society. Class Tickets are still used in England and are of great significance in the overseas missions of British Methodism.

70

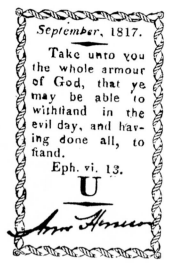

Methodist Class Tickets

—author's collection

The First Methodist Class Meeting, Bristol, 1742

The Foundry

THE first Methodist meetinghouse in London and the second in the world was the famous Foundry. It was a ruined factory for the casting of cannons, where the great bell of St. Paul's was cast. Repaired and remodeled, it was the headquarters of the Methodist movement for nearly forty years. Wesley acquired the property in 1739, and it became a chapel, residence, publishing house, savings bank, employment bureau, and a social center with a great variety of activities.

The Foundry, Moorfields, London

Newcastle

THE third Methodist center, following Bristol and London, was at Newcastle-on-Tyne, where Wesley established his Orphan House in 1742. It was his headquarters in the north of England. Like the New Room and the Foundry it housed many activities, though Wesley's original intention of developing there a home for orphans was not realized. But he kept a study at the Orphan House and here he did much of his writing and printing. One of the earliest Sunday schools was established in the center, and its choir became notable.

The Orphan House at Newcastle

Wesley's study at Newcastle

Beginning of Lay Preaching

THOMAS Maxfield, the first Methodist lay preacher, began preaching at the Foundry in London late in 1740 or early in 1741 while Wesley was absent at Bristol. Wesley was outraged and rushed to London for the purpose of silencing him. In a famous interview Susanna Wesley admonished her son to hear the young man and expressed the opinion that he was as truly called of God to preach as was Wesley himself. On hearing Maxfield, Wesley was convinced and withdrew his objections. Thus began lay preaching as an accepted Methodist policy.

—from Proceedings of Wesley Historical Society, March, 1949

Thomas Maxfield

The First Methodist Conference

THE first Methodist conference was held at the Foundry in London on June 25-30, 1744. Besides John and Charles Wesley, there were present four clergymen of the Church of England: John Hodges, Henry Piers, Samuel Taylor, and John Meriton. There were four lay preachers, John Downes, Thomas Maxfield, Thomas Richards, and John Bennet; of these only the first continued to the end as Methodist preachers. The subjects discussed were: (1) what to teach, (2) how to teach, and (3) what to do. Thus began the Methodist conference system.

The First Methodist Conference, London, June 25-30, 1744. Present were John and Charles Wesley, John Hodges, Henry Piers, Samuel Taylor, and John Meriton, all clergymen of the Church of England

The First Methodist Conference, 1744

The First Methodist Conference, 1744. The members of this historic conference were entertained in the London house of the Countess of Huntingdon
on Downing Street. John Wesley preached to the group on the theme, "What
hath God wrought!" Business was conducted by questions and answers, and this
remains true of Methodist conferences to this day.

The Methodist Society

TO counteract the spiritual decay of the times, "Religious Societies" sprang up in many places, often under Moravian auspices. It was in such a society that John Wesley was converted at Aldersgate. John Wesley adopted the idea, and his congregations or groups of members became Societies. The first was organized in Fetter Lane two or three weeks before the Wesleys experienced their spiritual awakening in 1738. In time Moravian influence became dominant in the Fetter Lane Society, and the doctrine of "stillness"—or disregard of the outward means of grace—led to its disruption. In 1740 John Wesley led his followers out of the Fetter Lane group and re-formed the Society at the Foundry.

Fetter Lane Chapel in 1867, built after Wesley moved away

Kingswood School

IT has been said that Methodism built a school before it built a church. The famous New Room at Bristol (1739) was at first called "The New Schoolhouse in the Horse-Fair"; it was a school with four masters and a mistress. The same was true of the Foundry at London (1739). Sixty children were taught there. But the first great educational enterprise of the Methodists, also in 1739, was a school for colliers' children at Kingswood. It was started and the cornerstone was laid by George Whitefield. In 1748 John Wesley opened at Kingswood a "New School," alongside the "Old School"; it was mainly for sons of the Methodist preachers. This Kingswood School was officially adopted by the Conference in 1756. In 1851 it was removed to the suburbs of Bath and remains as one of the finest of the Methodist schools.

Kingswood School

Kingswood School

—from Hurst

Scenes at the Kingswood School. *Upper left*, Wesley's oriel window; *upper right*, Wesley's walk; *center*, the gardens; *lower*, the main building

Death of Susanna Wesley

SUSANNA Wesley, the "Mother of Methodism," died in 1742 at the age of 73, at Foundry, where she spent the last years of her life. She was buried in the famous Bunhill Fields, across the City Road from Wesley's Chapel, near the tomb of John Bunyan. Her son John, standing by her open grave, preached her funeral sermon to a great congregation that he described as "one of the most solemn assemblies I ever saw, or expect to see on this side eternity."

HERE
lies the body of
MRS. SUSANNAH WESLEY
the youngest
and last surviving daughter of
Dr. Samuel Annesley
who died July 23, 1742
Aged 73 years

In sure and stedfast hope to rise,
And claim her mansion in the skies,
A Christian here her flesh laid down,
The cross exchanging for a crown.

True daughter of affliction she,
Inured to pain and misery,
Mourn'd a long night of grief and fears,
A legal night of seventy years.

The Father then reveal'd His Son,
Him in the broken bread made known.
She knew and felt her sins forgiven
And found the earnest of her Heaven.

Meet for the fellowship above,
She heard the call, "Arise, my Love."
"I come," her dying looks replied,
And lamb like as her Lord she died.

John Wesley at his Mother's grave in Bunhill Fields

Selina, Countess of Huntingdon. The associate and patroness of George Whitefield was the Right Honorable Selina, Countess of Huntingdon. Rich, influential, and deeply religious, she was virtually the secular head of the Calvinistic Methodists after Whitefield and others broke theologically with the Wesleys over the doctrine of predestination. The followers of the Calvinists are still active, especially in Wales.

Trevecca College. Lady Huntingdon founded chapels in various places. John Wesley preached in some of them occasionally, in spite of theological differences. Some of Wesley's outstanding preachers were drawn into her predestinarian circle, including, in addition to Whitefield, John Cennick, the first lay preacher, Howell Harris, and others. The Countess founded at Trevecca a training college for preachers in 1768, and Wesley supported it until 1771.

Trevecca House was the home of Howell Harris, one of Wesley's preachers who became a leader of the Calvinistic or predestinarian element among the early Methodists. Here the Welsh Methodists carried on for many years a religio-industrial community experiment, founded on an idea they derived from the Moravians and Count Zinzendorf's colony at Herrnhut in Germany.

—from an old print

Jean Guillaume de la Fletchere (1729-85). The saintly and scholarly John Fletcher was one of John Wesley's most devoted friends and an outstanding leader of early Methodism. He was born in Switzerland in 1729. Removing to England, he took orders in the Anglican Church in 1757 and was vicar of Madeley in Shropshire for a time. After joining Wesley he was superintendent of Trevecca College until Lady Huntingdon separated from Wesley. He became Wesley's foremost assistant and second in the Methodist command.

John Fletcher. Wesley's noble associate, John Fletcher, is known to fame and generations of theologians as the author of *Fletcher's Appeal*, a monumental work on sin and the Witness of the Spirit, the full title of which is *Appeal to Matter of Fact and Common Sense.*

John Fletcher

Madeley Church

John Fletcher

Fletcher's birthplace at Geneva

Mrs. John Fletcher was almost as well known and useful in Methodism as her husband. As Mary Bosanquet she was a Methodist preacher in her own right.

Mrs. Hester Ann Rogers, prominent in Methodism in the latter years of Wesley's life. Her journals and letters were read by thousands.

Reverend Joseph Benson, the "whirlwind" preacher, was one of the leading figures in the Methodist Conference, and twice its president, in the twenty-five years following the death of Wesley.

Reverend Henry Moore, close associate and helper of Wesley in his latter years, and subsequently his biographer. He also was twice president of the Conference in the early part of the nineteenth century.

John Nelson of Yorkshire was one of the early itinerant preachers often attacked by mobs.

Roland Hill (1744-1833), a popular preacher for half a century, was one of Wesley's Calvinistic opponents, writing attacks on him and on his doctrines. He introduced Sunday schools in London in 1786 and was one of the founders of the Religious Tract Society.

Timothy Hackworth, a prominent lay preacher, was a railway engineer, manager of the Stockton and Darlington railway from 1825, and an inventor.

James Hervey (1714-58), one of the Oxford Methodists and known throughout his life for his Christian piety, was one of the most popular writers of his day. He became a Calvinistic Methodist.

William Dawson (1773-1841), a yeoman farmer of Yorkshire, known as "Billy Dawson," was famous throughout England as a lay preacher of intellectual brilliance and dramatic eloquence.

—old print

Old time Sunday school

Hannah More (1745-1833), a poet and playwright, was associated with the literary circle of Johnson, Reynolds, Burke, and Garrick. She was an Evangelical Methodist, as was Hill, and wrote religious tracts, established Sunday schools, and engaged in numerous philanthropic activities.

Robert Raikes (1735-1811), a philanthropist, editor of the *Gloucester Journal,* raised the Sunday-school system into a national institution.

—old print

Old time Sunday school

—from Hurst

Barnabas Thomas, first superintendent
of the Wales Circuit, 1749

—from Hurst

Christopher Hopper, the first Wesleyan
itinerant preacher in Scotland

Charles Wesley

CHARLES WESLEY (1707-88), five years younger than his brother John, was cofounder of Methodism and fellow laborer with his brother. He accompanied John to Georgia and was spiritually awakened under Moravian influence one day before John Wesley's famous heartwarming Aldersgate experience. Charles Wesley went to Westminster School in London, of which his elder brother Samuel was junior master. In 1726 he went to Christ Church College at Oxford. Here he formed and was the first leader of the Holy Club, the original Methodist group. While at Westminster, Garrett Wesley of Ireland desired to adopt him; Charles refused and another boy was chosen, who became the ancestor of the Duke of Wellington.

Charles Wesley

91

Charles Wesley was one of the greatest hymn writers of all time and has around 6,500 poems to his credit. His "Wrestling Jacob," no longer found in the hymnal of American Methodism, has been widely acclaimed. Among his best-known and best-loved hymns are: "Hark, the Herald Angels Sing"; "Love Divine, All Loves Excelling"; "O for a Thousand Tongues to Sing"; "Come, Thou Almighty King"; "Christ the Lord Is Risen Today"; "Jesus, the Name High Over All"; "Arise, My Soul, Arise"; "O for a Heart to Praise My God"; "Soldiers of Christ, Arise"; "A Charge to Keep I Have"; and "Jesus, Lover of My Soul."

—from Hurst

Charles Wesley, Jr.

Dec. 18, 1748.

PROPOSALS

For PRINTING by SUBSRIPTION,

TWO VOLUMES

OF

Hymns and Sacred Poems.

By CHARLES WESLEY. M. A.
Student of *Chriſt-Church Oxford.*

CONDITIONS.

I. EACH Volume will contain upward of 300 Pages in large Duodecimo.

II. The Price of the Two Volumes will be 5*s.* half to be paid down, the reſt on the Delivery of the Books, in Quires.

III. The whole Work is ready for the Preſs, and will be Printed immediately.

IV. Bookſellers ſubſcribing for ſix Copies, will have a ſeventh Gratis.

SUBSCRIPTIONS are taken in by *T. Trye,* near *Gray's-Inn-Gate, Holbourn;* and at the *Foundry* in *Upper-Moor-Fields,* LONDON :—In *Newcaſtle upon Tyne,* by *R. Akenhead :*—In BRISTOL, by *Felix Farley,* in *Caſtle-Green; J. Wilſon,* Bookſeller, in *Wine-ſtreet.*
The SUSCRIBERS are deſired to ſend in their Names and Places of Abode.

Proposal for printing the hymns of Charles Wesley, 1794

—from an old print

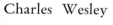

Charles Wesley

—from Hurst

Church in which Charles Wesley was married, a century after the event

Mrs. Sarah Wesley. Charles Wesley, priest of the Church of England, strongly opposed his brother's ordinations and all tendencies to break with the Anglicans. He also opposed John Wesley's love affair with Grace Murray and John's marriage to Mrs. Vazeille. Nevertheless, they remained in close association and affection. At the age of forty, Charles Wesley was married by his brother to Miss Sarah Gwynne, of a prominent Welsh family; their married life was long and happy, and their children were talented. Charles Wesley itinerated for several years but later settled down in parish work, first in Bristol and then in London.

Westminster School in Charles Wesley's time. *Upper left*, dormitory; *upper right*, school door; *center*, Little Dean's Yard; *Lower left*, old dormitory; *lower right*, great schoolroom.

Mrs. Charles Wesley

Charles Wesley, Jr., followed his father's footsteps and became an outstanding musician and London organist.

Sarah Wesley, daughter of Charles Wesley, was a talented poet and literary figure.

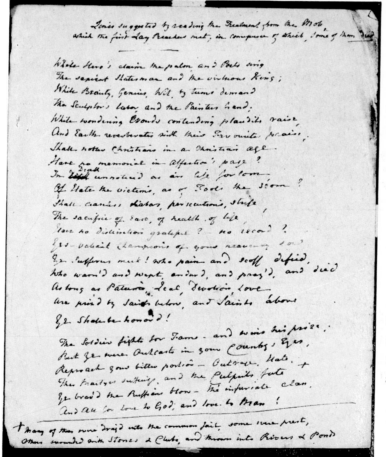

Sarah Wesley's poem on the persecutions of the early Methodist preachers, from the original manuscript in the author's collection.

Sarah Wesley's Tribute to the Early Methodist Preachers

While Hero's claim the palm and Poets sing
The sapient Statesman and the virtuous King;
While Beauty, Genius, Wit, by turns demand
The Sculptor's labor, and the Painters' hand;
While wondering Crowds contending plaudits raise,
And Earth reverberates with their Favourite praise;
Shall nobler Christians in a Christian age
Have no memorial in Affection's page?
In Death unnoticed as in life forlorn,
Of Hate the victims, as of Fools the scorn?
Shall ceaseless labors, persecutions, strife,
The sacrifice of ease, of health, of life,
Have no distinction grateful?—no record?
Yes—valiant Champions of your heavenly Lord,
Ye sufferers meek! who pain and scoff defied,
Who warm'd wept, endured, and pray'd, and died
As long as Patience, Zeal, Devotion, Love,
Are prized by Saints below, and Saints above
Ye shall be honored!
The soldier fights for Fame—and wins his prize;
But ye were Outcasts in your country's Eyes,
Reproach your bitter portion—Outrage, Hate.
The martyr's sufferings, and the culprit's fate
Ye brav'd the Ruffians blow—the infuriate clan,
And all for love to God, and love to Man!

Lines suggested by reading the Treatment from the Mob, which the
first Lay Preachers met; in consequence of which, some of them died

Statue of Charles Wesley, Bristol

Charles Wesley's tomb. Charles Wesley died on March 29, 1788, at the age of eighty years. So intense was his devotion to the Church of England, and so strong was his antipathy to John Wesley's ordinations and the Methodist trend away from Anglicanism, that he would not be buried in City Road churchyard, where his more famous brother rests. Charles Wesley was interred at Marylebone Church in London.

City Road Chapel

AFTER thirty-five years in the Foundry, John Wesley secured a site on City Road in London and erected City Road Chapel, which is looked upon as the Cathedral of British Methodism today. Seven thousand pounds were raised in three meetings, and contributions came from Methodists throughout Britain. Wesley laid the foundation stone in April, 1778, and the chapel was formally opened by Wesley on November 1, 1778.

The New Chapel, or Wesley's Chapel, City Road, London, opened in 1778

Wesley's Chapel, City Road, London

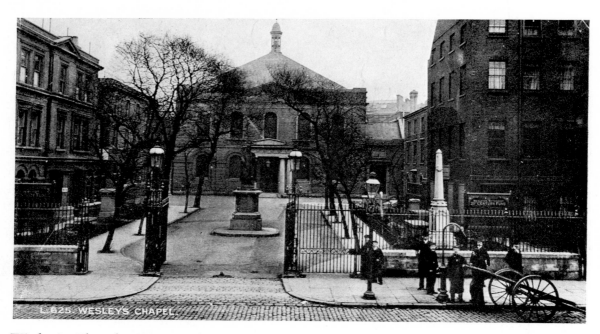

Wesley's Chapel, City Road, London. City Road was John Wesley's headquarters after 1778 until he died there in 1791. It is in use today. Adjacent is the publishing house of British Methodism. The Chapel was uninjured in World War II, though an adjoining church and much of the general area were demolished.

Interior of City Road Chapel, London   Wesley's Prayer Room, City Road

—from an old print in the author's collection

A composite picture showing John and Charles Wesley with more than four hundred Methodist preachers in City Road Chapel

The Deed of Declaration

IN 1784, the year that witnessed the organization of the Methodist Episcopal Church in America, John Wesley gave legal form to the Methodist movement in Great Britain, which had until that time been controlled by Wesley alone. He executed his famous Deed of Declaration, which provided that authority should be vested in a self-perpetuating body of one hundred preachers. The Legal Conference or the Hundred, and not the whole body of preachers and elected laymen, administers British Methodism to this day.

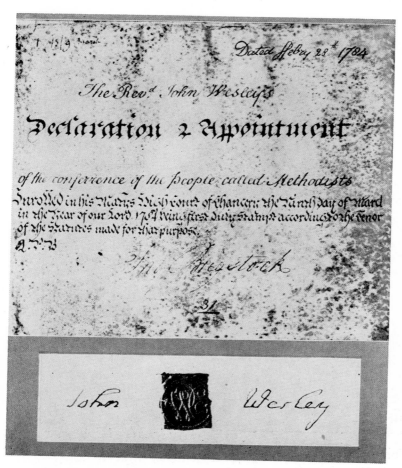

The last signature of John Wesley in the Journal of the Conference

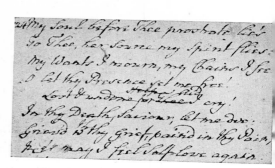

Endorsement to Wesley's Deed of Declaration, with his seal and signature

Manuscript of John Wesley's hymn, "My soul before Thee prostrate lies"

Wesley's Last Days

THE last letter written by John Wesley was addressed to William Wilberforce, the great reformer who was waging a fight against the slave trade. Wesley denounced the traffic as "the sum of all villanies" and urged Wilberforce to continue his campaign against it.

John Wesley and Wilberforce

John Wesley in his old age

N.B. For upwards of eighty-six years I have kept my accounts exactly. I will not attempt it any longer, being satisfied with the continual conviction that <u>I save all I can, and give all I can, that is, all I have.</u>

John Wesley
July 16, 1790

Last entry in John Wesley's account book, July 16, 1790

The tree under which John Wesley preached his last open-air sermon at Winchelsea

Death of John Wesley

JOHN WESLEY died in his house on City Road on March 2, 1791. He was attended by Dr. Whitehead, a physician, who preached his funeral sermon. Wesley's last words were, "I'll praise my Saviour while I've breath," and "The best of all is, God is with us." The picture shows all of those who were with or near him at the end, though not all of these were in the small room at one time.

The death of John Wesley

John Wesley Memorial Tablet, City Road, London

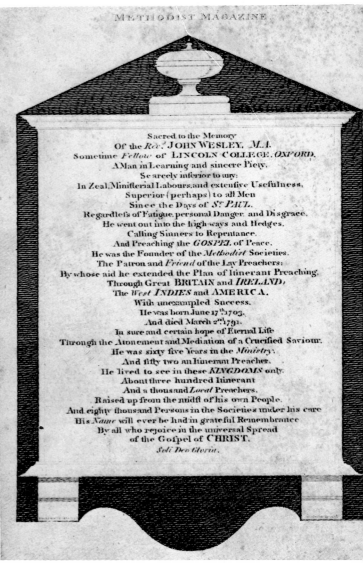

The statue of John Wesley, City Road, London

Death of John Wesley

JOHN WESLEY died in his house on City Road on March 2, 1791. He was attended by Dr. Whitehead, a physician, who preached his funeral sermon. Wesley's last words were, "I'll praise my Saviour while I've breath," and "The best of all is, God is with us." The picture shows all of those who were with or near him at the end, though not all of these were in the small room at one time.

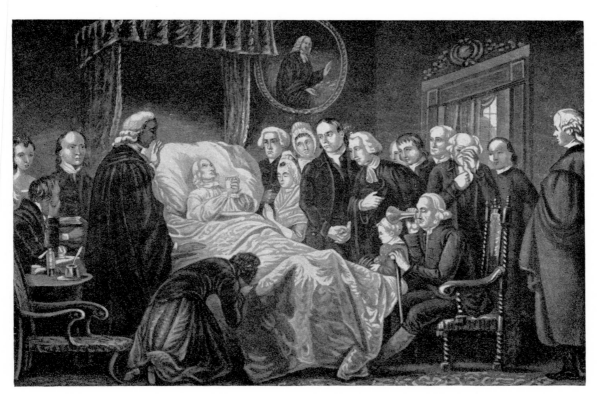

The death of John Wesley

The room in which John Wesley died

The funeral of John Wesley

—from an old print

The funeral of John Wesley

Wesley's grave at City Road Chapel, London

John Wesley Memorial Tablet, City Road, London

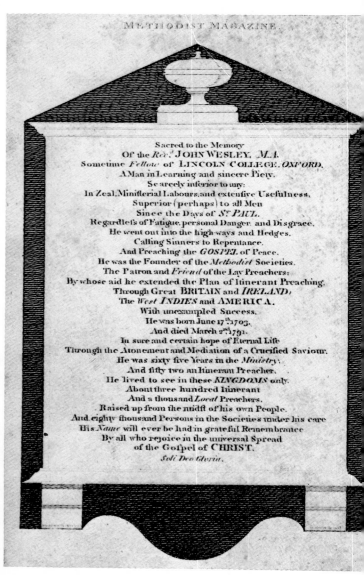

METHODIST MAGAZINE.

Sacred to the Memory
Of the Rev.ᵈ JOHN WESLEY, M.A.
Sometime Fellow of LINCOLN COLLEGE, OXFORD,
A Man in Learning and sincere Piety,
Scarcely inferior to any;
In Zeal, Ministerial Labours, and extensive Usefulness,
Superior (perhaps) to all Men
Since the Days of St PAUL,
Regardless of Fatigue, personal Danger, and Disgrace,
He went out into the high-ways and Hedges,
Calling Sinners to Repentance,
And Preaching the GOSPEL of Peace,
He was the Founder of the Methodist Societies,
The Patron and Friend of the Lay Preachers;
By whose aid he extended the Plan of Itinerant Preaching,
Through Great BRITAIN and IRELAND,
The West INDIES and AMERICA,
With unexampled Success.
He was born June 17ᵗʰ 1703,
And died March 2ᵈ 1791,
In sure and certain hope of Eternal Life
Through the Atonement and Mediation of a Crucified Saviour.
He was sixty five Years in the Ministry,
And fifty two an Itinerant Preacher,
He lived to see in these KINGDOMS only,
About three hundred Itinerant
And a thousand Local Preachers,
Raised up from the midst of his own People,
And eighty thousand Persons in the Societies under his care
His Name will ever be had in grateful Remembrance
By all who rejoice in the universal Spread
of the Gospel of CHRIST.
Soli Deo Gloria.

—from Methodist Ma

THE WORLD IS MY PARISH

The statue of John Wesley, City Road, London

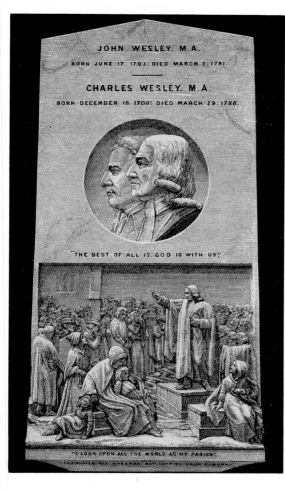

The Wesley Tablet in Westminster Abbey, the famous shrine where England's great are buried, quotes John Wesley's dying words, "The best of all is, God is with us," and his famous expression, "I look upon all the world as my parish." The bronze also shows Wesley preaching on his father's tomb at Epworth when he was excluded from the church.

Wesley Memorial Chapel at Epworth

Scenes in the life and work of John Wesley

Portraits of John Wesley

THE life of John Wesley covered nearly the whole of the eighteenth century (1703-91). At the beginning of his evangelical ministry he was shut out of the churches, assailed by press, pulpit, and pamphleteer, and physically assaulted by ruffians and even by their betters. He lived to see opposition melt away and himself become honored to the point of reverence. Across the years his fame has spread, and the movement which he started has belted the globe and become the largest free evangelical church on earth. Within weeks of his death a three-volume biography was published, and since that date more books have been written about him than about any other Englishman who ever lived, with the possible exception of Shakespeare. Men and women, friends and foes, Methodists, Anglicans, Jews, and Roman Catholics have written biographies of Wesley. Statues, portraits, busts, medals, statuettes, and art objects innumerable have been produced with his likeness. Probably there have been more portraits of John Wesley than any other Englishman, and painters continue to depict him. Here are reproduced a few Wesley portraits from the author's collection of prints.

The earliest known portrait of Wesley

John Wesley, Fellow of Lincoln College

111

John Wesley

John Wesley

114

"JOHN WESLEY"

—Jackson

"JOHN WESLEY"

—Barry

John Wesley

John Wesley at 63

—Romney

"JOHN WESLEY"

John Wesley

John Wesley at 87

John Wesley at 84

—Bartolozzi

"JOHN WESLEY"

This portrait is said to have been engraved by the famous engraver Bartolozzi, but it has also been declared spurious.

—Hunter

"JOHN WESLEY"

—John Kay

"JAMES HAMILTON, JOHN WESLEY, AND JOSEPH COLE"

This well-known print shows Wesley's small stature.

A rare old portrait of John Wesley

Mrs. John Wesley. John Wesley had two love affairs, the first with Sophy Hopkey in Georgia and the second with Grace Murray. In each case the romance was broken up. In 1751 Wesley married Mrs. Vazielle. The union was unhappy, owing to the lady's jealousy. In 1771 Wesley wrote in his *Journal*, "I was informed that my wife has left me. I did not send her away. I shall not bring her back." On October 12, 1781, he wrote, "I was informed that my wife died on Monday. This evening she was buried, though I was not informed of it till a day or two after."

Wesley's Successors

AFTER the death of Wesley the president of British Methodism was elected annually by the Conference. This usage still prevails.

William Thompson, first president of the Wesleyan Conference after the death of John Wesley, 1791.

Alexander Mather, second president of the Conference, 1792

John Pawson, third president of the Conference, 1793, and eleventh president, 1801

Adam Clarke was president of the Conference in 1806, 1814, and 1822. He was a great theological scholar, versed in sixteen languages, and the author of the famous *Clarke's Commentary*.

Richard Watson was president of the Conference in 1826. He wrote a life of Wesley, and his famous "Theological Institutes" were current for a century.

Jabez Bunting was president of the Conference in 1820, 1828, 1836, and 1844, the only man to serve four terms.

Benjamin Gregory, president of the Conference in 1879

James Dixon, president of the Conference in 1841

Luke H. Wiseman, president of the Conference in 1872

British Divisions and Reunion

AFTER the death of Wesley there arose in British Methodism demands for a complete break with the established church, the ordination of Methodist preachers, the administration of the sacraments, and the admission of laymen to the Conference. In 1795 the Conference adopted the "Plan of Pacification," which gave power to the preachers and allowed the sacraments to be administered, but continued dissension finally led to divisions and the organization of several branches of Methodism: Methodist New Connexion (1797), Independent Methodists (1806), Primitive Methodist Church (1811), Bible Christians (1810), Nonconforming or Protestant Methodists (1827), Wesleyan Reform Union (1849).

These controversies and schisms caused the loss of 100,000 members to Wesleyan Methodism. Then unification movements got under way. By the first part of the twentieth century there were three large Methodist bodies in Great Britain, the Primitive Methodists, United Methodists, and Wesleyan Methodists. These were united in 1932. Only a small group of Independent Methodist Churches and the Wesleyan Reform Union remained out of the unified body.

The British Methodist Church, including its missions, now has a membership of around 1,200,-000. The Independent Methodist Churches have 9,000 members, and the Wesleyan Reform Union has around 6,500. The churches are served by nearly 30,000 preachers, of which 25,000 are local preachers, including 2,500 women.

British Institutions

THE British Methodist Church has six theological schools: Richmond College, Richmond; Didsbury College, Bristol; Headingly College, Leeds; Handsworth College, Birmingham; Wesley House, Cambridge; Hartley-Victoria College, Manchester.

In addition, Cliff College near Sheffield trains lay evangelists, and Wesley Deaconess College at Ilkley, Yorkshire, provides training for the deaconesses.

Teacher training institutions are Westminster College for men and Southlands College for women, both in London. There are six residential schools for girls and eight for boys. There are independent residential schools under their own management: Queenswood School for girls near London; Kingswood School at Bath, the first and most historic of Methodist schools; Leys School in Cambridge. In addition there are more than one hundred day schools of various types. The National Children's Home and Orphanage, established in 1869, has forty homes which care for 4,000 children, and there are some Methodist Homes for the Aged.

121

Some British Methodist Theological Seminary Institutions

—early pictures from Hurst

From top to bottom: Richmond, Head-ingly, Didsbury, Handsworth

British Methodism Expands

JOHN WESLEY'S most famous words, "I look upon all the world as my parish," early found fulfillment as the Methodist movement leaped over the seas and established itself, first in America and then in other lands. This expansion was not originally the result of missionary planning but of the inherent spirit of the revival, for everywhere Methodism was carried by the evangelistic zeal of Methodists who emigrated from Great Britain.

British West Indies

NATHANIEL GILBERT and two Negro servants were converted by John Wesley during a visit to England, and they established Methodism in Antigua. Gilbert died in 1774, and the slaves continued the services. John Baxter arrived and took charge of the mission in 1778. Bishop Coke landed there in 1787, met Baxter, and incorporated the Antigua mission into the Methodist system.

Oldest Methodist church in Bermuda, at Hamilton, 1815

The first Mission at Kingston, Jamaica, 1789

Wesley conversing with a
Negro woman

—from Hurst

William Warrener, one of the pioneer
Wesleyan missionaries in the British
West Indies, Antigua, 1786

Joshua Marsden, an early Wesleyan missionary in Bermuda, 1808

—from Hurst

Nathaniel Gilbert preaching
in Antigua

Dr. Coke meeting John Baxter at Antigua, West Indies,
December 25, 1786

Beginnings on the Continent

THE noted John Fletcher returned to his native Switzerland and organized Methodist work there in 1777. Swiss Methodism later developed under the auspices of the American church. British Methodists preached in France in 1791, and a French Wesleyan Conference was formed in 1852. American Methodism entered France in 1907. Most of the churches later merged into the French Reformed Church.

William Toase, Wesleyan pioneer in France and general superintendent, 1818. He began preaching to French prisoners in a prison ship.

James Hocart (1812-90), Methodist pioneer in France and "Father of the French Conference"

The Southern Seas

BRITISH Methodists went to Australia as early as 1788. A Society was formed at Sydney in 1812 by Thomas Bowden, and Reverend Samuel Leigh was sent out from England in 1815. The work spread to Tasmania in 1820. Samuel Leigh pioneered among the cannibalistic Maoris in 1823, and Samuel Marston and Walter Lawry followed him in New Zealand. Methodists entered the Friendly Islands in 1822 and the Fiji Islands in 1832. Today 90 per cent of the Fijians are Methodists, and the baptismal font at Bau is made from the stone on which the skulls of human victims were once crushed. Methodism now occupies a dominant position in the South Pacific.

First Mission Station in New Zealand

First Mission House at Tonga, Fiji Islands

First Mission House at Veva, Fiji Islands

Reverend Samuel Marsden, one of the founders of Methodism in New Zealand, 1823

Reverend Samuel Leigh, first Wesleyan missionary and virtual founder of Methodism in Australia, 1815, and also in New Zealand, 1823

Reverend James Calvert, Wesleyan missionary in the Fiji Islands, 1838-55 and 1860-65

—from Hurst

Reverend Walter Lawry, Methodist pioneer in Australia, 1818
and superintendent of the New
Zealand mission, 1844

—from Hurst

—from Hurst

Reverend John Thomas, missionary at Tonga, in the Friendly Islands, 1824

—from Hurst

Reverend Peter Turner, missionary in the Friendly Islands and Samoa, 1834

Peter VI, first native preacher in Polynesia, about 1830

Africa

BRITISH Methodism entered Sierra Leone as early as 1795 and in later years spread to South Africa, Gambia, the Gold Coast, the Ivory Coast, Nigeria, Dahomey and Togoland, Kenya, Fernando Po, and Rhodesia.

—from Hurst

Reverend Thomas B. Freeman, pioneer Wesleyan missionary in West Africa and famous "ambassador to the Ashantis" of the Gold Coast, 1838. He ranged far and wide and was largely responsible for the strong Methodism that now exists under British auspices in West Africa.

—from Hurst

Reverend William Shaw, pioneer Wesleyan
missionary in Kaffirland, South Africa, 1820

—from Hurst

Reverend Barnabas Shaw, pioneer Wesleyan missionary in
South Africa, 1816, the first Methodist missionary at the
Cape of Good Hope

Asia

THOMAS COKE died in 1814 while en route to Ceylon with a party of Wesleyan missionaries and was buried in the Indian Ocean. His party proceeded and established Methodism there. The Dam Street Methodist Church in Colombo is the oldest Methodist church in all Asia. Wesleyan Methodists went to China in 1851 and to Burma in 1887. When the independent Church of South India was formed in 1947 the British Methodists contributed to the merger 1,560 churches and 230,000 members.

The first Wesleyan Missionaries' Home in Mandalay, Burma, 1887. It was a former Buddhist Monastery.

The oldest Methodist Church in Asia, Colombo

133

SECTION 2

American Methodism

FRANCIS ASBURY (1745-1816)

"The Prophet of the Long Road," creator and directing spirit of American Methodism, was to America what John Wesley was to Britain.

GEORGE WHITEFIELD arrived in America soon after John Wesley departed, and the continent then became a favorite scene of his labors. Seven times he visited the New World, preaching Calvinistic Methodism from New England to Georgia. Shut out of the churches, he preached in the open air. As he preached on the courthouse steps at Philadelphia, Benjamin Franklin estimated that he could have been heard by 30,000 people.

—from Billingsley

George Whitefield preaching on the courthouse steps at Philadelphia, 1739

138

—John Woolaston, *National Portrait Gallery, London*

"GEORGE WHITEFIELD"

—from Billingsley

Whitefield's great field victory—350 conversions in one sermon

Whitefield's Orphan House, Savannah. George Whitefield founded the Bethesda Orphanage at Savannah, and it is still in operation. He laid the first brick on March 25, 1740, and raised money for the institution in America and England.

Whitefield also started a school for Negroes at Nazareth, in Pennsylvania. Peter Böhler and other Moravians worked on the building, which was later purchased and finished by them and is now a home for Moravian missionaries.

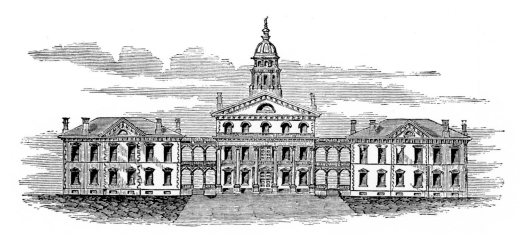

New Orphan House, Savannah

—from Hurst

The Old South Presbyterian Church, Newburyport, Massachusetts. George Whitefield was buried under its altar

Whitefield Monument at the University of Pennsylvania. In 1740 Whitefield began the erection at 62 North Fourth Street, Philadelphia, of a church and charity school known as the "New Building" and the Academy. This was later purchased when the rented building in which Franklin and others started an academy was outgrown, and here began the University of Pennsylvania. An inscription on the monument reads: "The University of Pennsylvania held its first sessions in a building erected for his congregations and was aided by his collections, guided by his counsels, inspired by his life."

George Whitefield at 29

Whitefield's last exhortation on the stairway of the house in which he died at Newburyport, Massachusetts, Sunday morning, September 30, 1770

Methodism Established in America

ARMINIAN Methodism came to the New World without previous design, for Wesley had taken no steps to send a missionary. But some of his preachers came voluntarily, and the Methodist movement began under their evangelistic efforts. Robert Strawbridge, an immigrant from Ireland, started the work in Maryland. Philip Embury, also from Ireland, founded Methodism in New York. Captain Thomas Webb, of the British army, was responsible for its origin in Philadelphia. Uncertainty exists as to whether the movement began first in Maryland or in New York.

Methodism in Maryland

BORN at Drumsna in Ireland and almost certainly converted there under the preaching of John Wesley, Robert Strawbridge came to Maryland in 1759 or 1760 and settled on Sam's Creek in Frederick County. He built a log house and began preaching. He organized a class of six members, meeting alternately in his own home and in the home of John England, and soon started another at the home of Andrew Poulson. In 1763 or 1764 the two classes were merged and organized into a society. Strawbridge preached, baptized his converts, formed circuits, appointed preachers, and administered the Holy Communion in spite of protests from both Wesley and Asbury.

Robert Strawbridge

Old John Evans House. Strawbridge's first sermons were probably preached here, since John Evans, along with Andrew Poulson, Benjamin Marcarel, and John England, was a member of the first society organized.

Strawbridge's log meetinghouse. This log house, 24 by 24 feet in size, is said to have been erected about 1764. It gave way to a better house on Pipe Creek, called Poulson's Chapel, in 1783. In 1800 a stone church took its place, and there Bishops Asbury and Whatcoat held a conference in 1801. At that time Asbury wrote in his journal: "This settlement of Pipe Creek is the richest in the State; here Mr. Strawbridge formed the first Society in Maryland—*and America.*"

The house where Strawbridge died (1781) and where his funeral was held

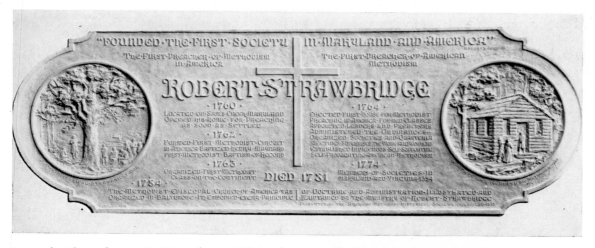

Strawbridge plaque in Maryland. This plaque calls Strawbridge "the first preacher of Methodism in America" and "the first preacher of American Methodism." It points to the high points of his career: 1760—located on Sam's Creek and began preaching; 1762—formed the first circuit in America and baptized Henry Maynard, the first baptism on record; 1763—organized the first Methodist class on the continent; 1764—built the first house of worship.

It is said that Robert Strawbridge during his ministry converted and raised up more Methodist preachers than any other preacher of his generation in America. Many of these became Methodism's outstanding leaders. Among them were Philip Gatch, William Watters, Henry Maynard, Richard Owings, Freeborn Garrettson, and Daniel Ruff.

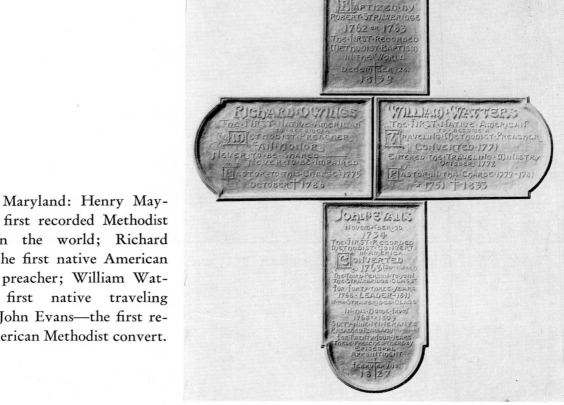

Plaque in Maryland: Henry Maynard—the first recorded Methodist baptism in the world; Richard Owings—the first native American Methodist preacher; William Watters—the first native traveling preacher; John Evans—the first recorded American Methodist convert.

Bush Forest Chapel, Maryland, erected in 1768, the second or third in America

The Stone Chapel, which replaced Strawbridge's log meetinghouse, 1800

Holden's Meetinghouse, Queen Anne County, Maryland, built around 1775 and one of the oldest in the state

P

HILIP EMBURY, founder of Methodism in New York, was born at Ballingrane, Ireland, on December 25, 1728, among German refugees from the Rhine Palatinate referred to by John Wesley as "about the lowest type of an irreligious, swearing, drunken community that I have ever met." He was converted under Wesley's preaching, became a local preacher, and in 1760 sailed for America, landing at New York on August 1. With him were three brothers, a sister, and a cousin, with their families.

Philip Embury

Extract from Embury's notebook: "On Christmas Day; being Monday ye 25th day of December, in the year of 1752; the Lord Shone into my Soul by a glimpse of His Redeeming love; being an earnest of my redemption in Christ Jesus, to whom be glory for ever and ever. Amen. Phil: Embury."

Barbara Heck. The Methodists from Ireland were religiously negligent in America. Barbara Heck, Embury's cousin, was dramatically responsible for the first Methodist sermon in New York.

Philip Embury preaching to Palatines when leaving Limerick for America, 1760

—John Cassel

"BARBARA HECK AND THE CARD PLAYERS"

In 1766 Barbara Heck found a group engaged in card playing. She seized the cards and threw them into the fire, roundly rebuking the backsliders. Rushing to Embury's house the good lady cried out, "Philip, you must preach to us, or we shall all go to hell, and God will require our blood at your hands."

"How can I preach?" replied Embury. "I have neither house nor congregation."

"Preach," said Mrs. Heck, "in your own house, and to your own company."

—Dan Beard from Hurst

"BARBARA HECK EXHORTING PHILIP EMBURY TO PREACH THE GOSPEL"

Philip Embury's house in New York. Embury preached the first Methodist sermon in his rented house at 10 Augustus Street in the autumn of 1766.

Philip Embury preaching the first Methodist sermon in New York. The members of the first class formed in New York were Embury and his wife, Paul and Barbara Heck, John Lawrence, and Betty, a Negro servant.

Captain Thomas Webb

WHEN Embury's house became crowded, a room was rented near the barracks, "in the worst section of the town." At the close of a service a man in uniform strode forward and introduced himself: "Captain Thomas Webb, of the King's service, and also a soldier of the cross and a spiritual son of John Wesley." He became a leader in the Methodist movement and the founder of Methodism in Philadelphia.

Captain Thomas Webb

—J. Carter Beard from Hurst

"CAPTAIN THOMAS WEBB ON A MISSIONARY EXCURSION"

The Rigging Loft

IN 1767 the Methodists rented a sailmaker's attic at 120 William Street, and here they worshiped under the ministry of Embury and Webb. The former soon settled near Salem, New York, where he preached until his death in August, 1773. Barbara Heck moved to Canada and died there in 1801. Captain Webb preached in various places in America. He returned to England in 1778 and died near Bristol on December 20, 1796.

The Rigging Loft in New York

Captain Webb preaching in the
Rigging Loft

John Street Church

THE first Methodist building in New York was erected on John Street in 1768. Called Wesley Chapel, it was "a substantial one of stone, faced with blue plaster, 60 by 42 feet, and was provided with a chimney and fireplace." There was a gallery, reached by a ladder. The building cost between 600 and 800 pounds. Much of the money was raised by Captain Webb. On the subscription paper, which is still preserved, are the names of prominent citizens, the mayor of the city, and some African slaves. Embury dedicated the chapel on October 30, 1768.

John Street Church and Parsonage

The second John Street Church, 1818

The third John Street Church, 1841. A Methodist church has stood on the John Street lot from 1768 until the present day. It is one of the shrines of American Methodism. Asbury and all the early Methodist preachers preached there.

Methodism in Philadelphia

IT IS said that the first Methodist preacher in Philadelphia was Edward Evans, one of George Whitefield's converts, 1739 or 1740. Organized Methodism began in a sail loft, where James Emerson gathered a class around 1767. Captain Webb found the group that year and organized a society of seven members, thus becoming the founder of Philadelphia Methodism. On November 23, 1769, the society purchased an unfinished Dutch Reformed church for 650 pounds. This was St. George's Church, the first Methodist building in the world to be called a church, the oldest Methodist meetinghouse on the continent.

St. George's Church, Philadelphia, 1769

Bishop Asbury Preaching in St. George's Church, Philadelphia

Coming of the Missionaries

TWO other unofficial Methodist preachers came to America: Robert Williams in 1768 and John King in 1769. In August, 1769, the English conference met at Leeds. Wesley reported: "We have a pressing call from our brethren of New York (who have built a meetinghouse) to come over and help them. Who is willing to go?" Richard Boardman and Joseph Pilmoor volunteered and became the first missionaries. With passage money provided and with fifty pounds for the debt on the John Street building, they landed at Gloucester Point, below Philadelphia, on October 24, 1769.

Richard Boardman   Joseph Pilmoor

Old Boggard House, Leeds, England, where the conference met in 1769 and where the first two missionaries volunteered for America

The Great Asbury

AT the Bristol Conference in 1771 Wesley again called for volunteers for America. Five preachers responded, and Wesley chose two, Richard Wright and Francis Asbury. The latter never returned to England, but virtually created The Methodist Church and became the greatest figure of its history. Asbury and Wright sailed on September 4, 1771, and landed at Philadelphia on October 27. On board the ship Asbury began his famous *Journal,* the most important literary work of American Methodism. On September 12 he wrote: "Whither am I going? To the New World. What to do? To gain honor? No, if I know my own heart. To get money? No, I am going to live to God and to bring others so to do."

Francis Asbury

Elizabeth Asbury, mother of
Francis Asbury

Asbury's birthplace, "near the foot of Hampstead Bridge, in the parish of
Handsworth, about four miles from Birmingham in Staffordshire"

Francis Asbury

Francis Asbury, from the "Methodist Magazine," London, 1809. Asbury arrived 150 years after other churches, but under his leadership Methodism outstripped them all. When he came, there were a dozen preachers; when he died, there were 695. He ordained 4,000 by his own hands. During his ministry the number of Methodists grew from 1,200 persons, who were members of no church and had no ordained or ecclesiastically recognized ministry, to 214,000 members of a fully organized, widely extended and flourishing church with nine annual conferences. The ratio growth of Methodism far surpassed the growth of the population.

Mr. F. ASBURY.

General Superintendent of the Methodist Societies in the United States of America

—from Hurst

Manwood Cottage, Handsworth, England, where Asbury first preached

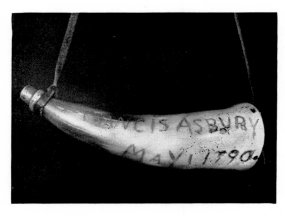

Bishop Asbury's powder horn, in the museum at John Street Church, New York

—from an old print

Asbury beginning his itinerant ministry. Asbury held a watch-night service and preached in St. George's at Philadelphia and then proceeded to New York, preaching along the way. On November 20 he wrote in his *Journal:* "My brethren seem unwilling to leave the cities, but I think I will show them the way." He did. Greatest of the itinerants, he rode on horseback or in a carriage 270,000 miles and preached 16,000 times. More than sixty times he crossed the uncharted Appalachians. He never had a home, a boarding place, or an address save "America." He died by the side of the road he traveled, and in his last delirium he tried to take a missionary collection.

The First American Conference

THE appointments made at the first American conference were: New York, Thomas Rankin (to change in four months); Philadelphia, George Shadford (to change in four months); Baltimore, Francis Asbury, Robert Strawbridge, Abraham Whitworth, Joseph Yearby; New Jersey, John King, William Watters; Petersburg, Robert Williams. After the conference Rankin appointed Philip Gatch in Watters' place.

—from an old print

At the first American Conference, Philadelphia, 1773

—from Hurst

The Old Court House at Salem, New Jersey, where Daniel Ruff preached the first Methodist sermon in the town

Thomas Rankin. In 1772 Wesley sent two additional missionaries to America, Thomas Rankin and George Shadford.

George Shadford. Wesley wrote: "I let you loose, George, on the great continent of America. Publish your message in the open face of the sun."

Methodists Ride the Seaboard

THE first conference in 1773 was the beginning of organized Methodism, but eleven years were to pass before it became a church. On December 8, 1769, Pilmoor inaugurated at St. George's, Philadelphia, the "Intercession" or prayer meeting; on March 23, 1770, he held there the first love feast; on November 1 he conducted the first watch night. These became fixed customs among the Methodists.

In England a new appointment appeared in the conference minutes in 1770: "No. 150—America."

Robert Williams rode South and introduced Methodism in Virginia, preaching his first sermon in 1772 on the courthouse steps at Norfolk and converting Isaac Luke, a prominent businessman at Portsmouth. Williams was followed by Pilmoor, Boardman, Watters, and Asbury. In 1774 Williams formed the Brunswick circuit, and that year James Dempster, Martin Rodda, and William Glendenning arrived from England to reinforce the seventeen preachers.

The second conference at Philadelphia in 1774 reported 2,073 members, and at the third conference the following year there were 3,148. Now there were circuits from New York to Norfolk. Both Embury and Williams died that year; the latter was "the first to publish a book, to marry, and to locate."

John King preached the first Methodist sermon in Baltimore in 1770 on a block in front of a blacksmith shop at Front and Center streets

Freeborn Garrettson preaching in Dorchester County jail, Maryland

The German Church, Baltimore. Philip Otterbein, Asbury's friend and in 1800 one of the founders and one of the first bishops of the United Brethren Church, ministered here, and here Pilmoor "joined together" the first class in Baltimore in 1772.

—from Hurst

Parsonage of the famous old Light Street Church in Baltimore

Strawberry Alley, the first Methodist chapel started in Baltimore, in 1773, where the Dallas Street Church now stands. The class was organized by Asbury previously.

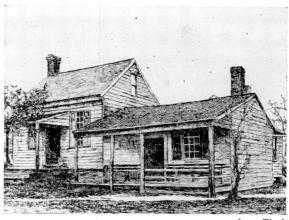

—from Tipple

"Black Harry" Hoosier, Methodist Negro evangelist who frequently accompanied Asbury on preaching tours

House at Petersburg, Virginia, where Methodist services were held and where the first conference in Virginia met. Robert Williams was appointed pastor at Petersburg at the first conference in 1773.

—from Hurst

Old Capitol, Williamsburg, Virginia, where Pilmoor preached in 1772

Freeborn Garrettson. Converted in 1775 by Strawbridge at the age of 23, he was a leading preacher until his death in 1827. He married Miss Katherine Livingston, whose eldest brother, Chancellor Robert Livingston, administered the oath of office to President George Washington.

The American Revolution

IN the American Revolution the Methodists were regarded as Tories. All the preachers sent over by Wesley, save Asbury alone, returned to England; Asbury was ordered back, but he refused to go. In 1775 Wesley wrote his "Calm Address to Our American Colonies," in which he rehearsed Dr. Samuel Johnson's attack on the Americans, and this did much damage, but Asbury remained. Once he was fined for preaching. For over a year he was secluded in the home of Judge Thomas White in Delaware.

Perry Hall, home of Henry Dorsey Gough, near Baltimore. Gough, a man of wealth, was converted in 1775, and his home was a preaching place and open to the preachers. Asbury preached here after the Declaration of Independence. Gough built a chapel near his house which was the first meetinghouse that had a bell.

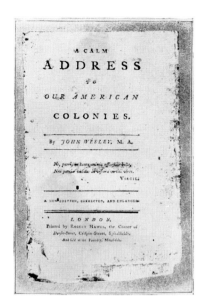

Wesley's "Calm Address to
Our American Colonies"

"MRS. HENRY DORSEY GOUGH"—Jarvis

—from Hurst

Reverend Major Thomas Morrell, who
with John Dickins waited upon President George Washington and arranged
for him to receive Bishops Coke and
Asbury

After the Revolution

IN both England and America the subordination of the Methodists caused trouble. The followers of Wesley, who had no other church connections, demanded the ordinances of baptism, marriage, and the holy sacraments at the hands of their preachers. This the Wesleys and Asbury resisted. The question was raised in all the conferences of the period. Strawbridge refused to be bound by restrictions. In 1775-76 the first Methodist revival in America swept through Virginia. In 1779 the Virginia preachers revolted, and in a conference at Broken Back Church, Fluvanna County, ordained each other and decided to administer the ordinances. There was a breach in the Methodist body, between the northern and the southern preachers, but a temporary truce was patched up. The main issue, however, could not be ignored.

—Potts

Marker on the site of the Broken Back Church, in Fluvanna County, Virginia. In this church in 1779 the Methodist preachers ordained each other and decided to administer the ordinances in spite of orders to the contrary.

—Potts

Sign marking the site of Mason's Chapel, in Fluvanna County, Virginia, on the spot near which the preachers revolted in 1779 on the question of administering the ordinances

Wesley's Decisive Step

SOMETHING had to be done about the ordinances, and the Church of England refused to ordain Methodist preachers. Lord Peter King's book on the Primitive Church convinced Wesley that there are but two orders, and that he, as a presbyter, had the same right as a bishop to ordain. He proceeded to act. In September, 1784, at Bristol, he consecrated Dr. Thomas Coke as "superintendent" for America and Richard Whatcoat and Thomas Vasey as presbyters, and authorized them to ordain others and administer the ordinances. The decisive step was taken in the house of Dr. Castelman, a physician and Wesley's friend, at No. 6 Dighton Street, "a little up the hill from Charles Wesley's house in Charles Street."

Title page of King's "Enquiry," which convinced Wesley that episcopacy is not a distinct order, and that he, as a presbyter, had authority to ordain

A N
ENQUIRY
INTO THE
Conſtitution, Diſcipline, Unity and Worſhip,
OF THE
Primitive Church,
That Flouriſh'd within the firſt Three Hundred Years after CHRIST.

Faithfully Collected out of the Extant Writings of thoſe Ages.

By an Impartial Hand.

L O N D O N,
Printed for *J. Wyat* at the *Roſe,* and *R. Robinſon* at the *Golden-Lyon,* in St. *Paul's Church-Yard.* 1713.

173

Richard Whatcoat   Thomas Vasey

James Creighton, presbyter of the
Church of England, who, with John
Wesley, laid hands on Dr. Thomas
Coke, Richard Whatcoat, and
Thomas Vasey

—from Hurst

Dr. Lowth, Bishop of London, who refused Wesley's request to ordain Methodist preachers for America and thus became responsible for the final rupture between Methodism and the Church of England

Three preachers were ordained by John Wesley in City Road Chapel in 1785. Thomas Hanby, Joseph Taylor, John Pawson

Wesley ordained eighteen preachers. Alexander Mather he explicitly ordained a bishop, and he ordained Henry Moore "to administer the sacraments of baptism and the Lord's Supper according to the usages of the Church of England." All this scandalized Charles Wesley. On the ordination of Coke he wrote this "Epigram":

W— himself and friends betrays,
By his good sense forsook,
While suddenly his hands he lays
On the hot head of C—.

Yet we at least should spare the weak,
His weak coevals we,
Nor blame an hoary schismatic,
A saint of eighty-three.

So easily are bishops made
By man's or woman's whim!
W— his hands on C— has laid,
But who laid hands on Him!

Hands on himself he laid, and took
An apostolic chair;
And then ordained his creature C—
His heir and successor.

Thomas Coke

THOMAS COKE, LL.D. of Oxford, was the first Protestant bishop in America, though he was never elected to the office and was designated by Wesley as "superintendent." He was a scholar and voluminous writer, and with Henry Moore published Wesley's biography in 1792. Called the "Foreign Minister of Methodism," Coke crossed the Atlantic eighteen times and was the father of Methodist missions. He prepared plans for a missionary society in 1784, nine years before Carey went to India. He was a man of means, and at his own expense he founded missions among the French and in the West Indies. He died on the way to Ceylon and was buried in the Indian Ocean.

Certificate of Thomas Coke. Wesley's ordinations have been debated to this day. They denied "apostolic succession" and set up episcopacy as an office but not an order. They took Methodism forever out of the State Church, ritualistic, and priestly system.

Thomas Coke (1747-1814)

Coke's letter to Fletcher transmitting the plan for a Methodist missionary society

Dr. Thomas Coke

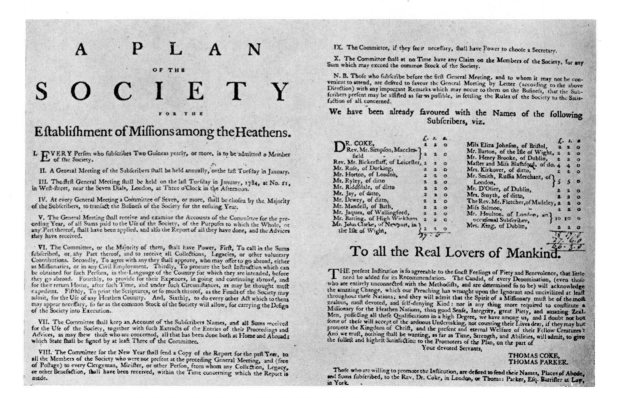

Coke's plan for a Methodist missionary society, 1784

ASBURY "was greatly surprised to see Brother Whatcoat assist by taking cup" in the Communion service, after Coke's sermon. He was "shocked" when he learned that Coke proposed to consecrate him and declined to accept consecration as superintendent unless elected by the preachers. Freeborn Garrettson "rode off like an arrow" to summon the preachers, while Coke went on a thousand-mile preaching tour.

Barratt's Chapel. At Barratt's Chapel, twelve miles from Dover, Delaware, a memorable meeting between Coke and Asbury occurred on November 14, 1784. This chapel still stands and has been designated as a shrine of Methodism. The floor was laid, rough seats arranged, and Asbury merged from his war exile to officiate at the first quarterly conference in the structure in November, 1780.

Interior of Barratt's Chapel

Organization of the Methodist Church

LOVELY Lane Chapel, Baltimore, was erected in 1774. The class was formed by Asbury in 1772. On December 24, 1784, the famous Christmas Conference met in Lovely Lane Chapel, with sixty-three of the eighty-four preachers present. On motion of John Dickins the societies were given the name "Methodist Episcopal Church." Thomas Coke and Francis Asbury were set apart as general superintendents. They called themselves "bishops" over the protest of John Wesley. Thus "there came to birth in America, in a republic without a constitution and without a President, the first Methodist Episcopal Church in the world." The unordained lay preachers for the first time invested with the office that commanded legal recognition and public respect.

Lovely Lane Chapel, Baltimore

Plaque on the site of Lovely
Lane Chapel, Baltimore

The Christmas Conference

THE Christmas Conference adopted the first Methodist *Discipline* and accepted a shortened form of worship sent over by Wesley. One of its first questions was: "What may be reasonably expected to have been God's design in raising up the Methodist preachers?" The answer has been one of American Methodism's watchwords: "To reform the continent and spread scriptural holiness over these lands." It adopted instructions to preachers which remain unrepealed, such as "Never be unemployed. Never be triflingly employed. Neither spend more time in any place than is strictly necessary." It set the annual salary of all preachers, including Asbury, at "$64 and no more."

The Upper Room in Lovely Lane Chapel, where the Christmas Conference met in 1784

An early Conference in Baltimore

—from Tipple

The consecration of Bishop Asbury

The consecration of Bishop Asbury. On Christmas day, 1784, Coke, assisted by Whatcoat and Vasey, ordained Francis Asbury as a deacon. The next day he was ordained an elder. On the third day he was consecrated as a superintendent of the Methodist Episcopal Church.

—from an old print

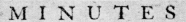

Minutes of the Christmas Conference. Foreign missions was born with the church. The Christmas Conference sent Freeborn Garrettson and James O. Cromwell to Nova Scotia and Jeremiah Lambert to the West Indies. Methodist education was similarly born. Cokesbury College was launched by preachers who had little or no formal education.

—from the Clark collection

Dr. Coke's unfinished circular on the Methodist missions in the West Indies

Signatures of early Methodist leaders in England and America

—from Clark's *The Wesley Family*

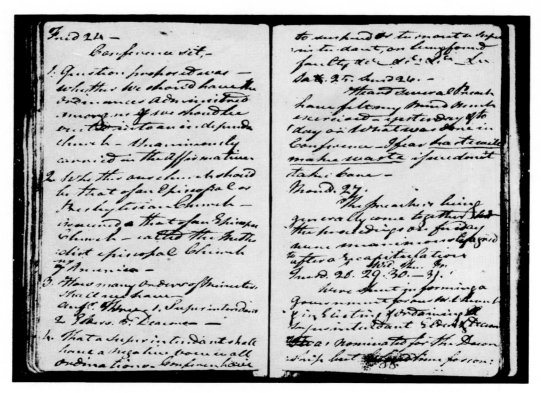

Pages from the diary of Thomas Haskins describing the Christmas Conference. This manuscript is in the Library of Congress at Washington. "You have nothing to do but save souls," declared the Christmas Conference. "You are not to preach so many times, or take care of this or that society but to save as many souls as you can. . . . Your duty is to bring as many sinners as you possibly can to repentance, and with all your power to build them up in that holiness without which they cannot see the Lord."

The New Church

THE new church had eighty-three preachers, forty-three circuits, and 14,988 members along the seaboard from New York to North Carolina. Its main strength was in the South. Only 2,589 members were found north of Maryland, and none north of Long Island Sound. There was but one conference, which met in three sections. In 1788 there were six sections, and by 1792 there were seventeen. In 1792 the "general conference" was created. In 1796 six separate annual conferences were formed.

Henry Willis, the first preacher ordained by Bishop Asbury

The six annual conferences formed
in 1796: New England, Philadelphia,
Baltimore, Virginia, Western, and
South Carolina

Asbury's Episcopal Round in 1788. Asbury rode this wide circuit and held all the conferences each year.

The Work Spreads

—A. W. Potts

St. Peter's Church, near Thomas Crenshaw's place in Hanover County, Virginia, successor to the church where in 1786 Asbury organized what has been called the first Sunday school in America

188

The home of Green Hill, near Louisburg, North Carolina, where on April 20, 1785, was held the first conference after the organization of the church. Coke and Asbury were both present. Hill later moved to Tennessee, and in his home near Nashville, Bishop McKendree held the Western Conference in 1808.

Wakefield, the home of Henry Willis, on Pipe Creek, Maryland. He was the first preacher ordained by Asbury. The Baltimore Conference met here in 1801.

—J. Manning Potts

Marker at the site of Mason's Chapel in Brunswick County, Virginia, where Asbury held the first Virginia Conference in 1785

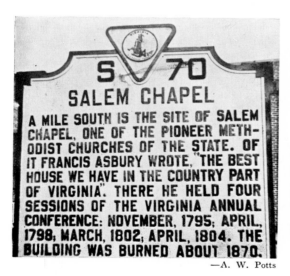

—A. W. Potts

Marker near the site of Salem Chapel, South Hill, Virginia, called "the best house we have in the country part of Virginia," and where he held conferences in 1795, 1798, 1802, and 1804

Old Ebenezer, erected in 1790, the first church built by the Methodists in Philadelphia. St. George's was purchased from another denomination.

Rehoboth Methodist Church, Union, West Virginia, erected in 1785. Asbury dedicated it in 1786 and held conferences there in 1792, 1793, and 1796.

The Old Tobacco House, Washington, D. C., where Methodist services were held from 1807 to 1811. An eminent Methodist, Henry Foxall, built the first Foundry Chapel, which developed into the present Foundry Church, in Washington, out of gratitude because his foundry had been spared when the British burned the city in 1814.

—from Hurst

Ebenezer Methodist Church, Washington, D. C., erected in 1811. It is said that the noted Thomas O. Summers was converted here.

—from Hurst

Old Wesley Chapel, Savannah, Georgia, dedicated by Bishop Asbury in 1813

—from Hurst

Methodist Education

THE Christmas Conference ordered the uneducated Methodist preachers to "instruct the children in every place," an order which still stands. Furthermore, they were to preach annually on education, and the instructions were firm: "But I have no gift for this." "Gift or no gift, you are to do it, else you are not called to be a Methodist preacher." Consequently, American Methodism has covered the land with educational institutions and operates more schools than any other Protestant body.

Ebenezer Academy, Brunswick County, Virginia, the first Methodist school in America. It was founded some time between 1783 and 1793 and antedates Cokesbury College.

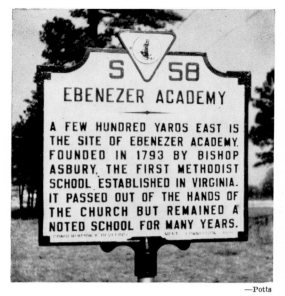

—Potts

—Potts

Marker near site of Ebenezer Academy   Ruins of Ebenezer Academy

Elizabeth Academy, near Washington, Mississippi, one of the earliest schools of Methodism in America, founded in 1819

Cokesbury College, the first Methodist College in America, was named for Bishops Coke and Asbury. Funds were in hand when the Christmas Conference met in 1784, and it was formally opened by Asbury on December 8-10, 1787. It was located near Abingdon in Maryland. It was incorporated and authorized to confer degrees in 1794. In 1795 the building was destroyed by fire. A second Cokesbury was opened in a building adjoining the Light Street Church in Baltimore, and this was burned in 1796. Asbury College was opened in Baltimore in 1816, but it died "for want of money and of a mongrel religion," several of its teachers being non-Methodists.

Marker near the site of Cokesbury College

—Alpheus W. Potts

Old Randolph-Macon College at Boydton, Virginia. Opened in 1832, it is now one of the oldest Methodist colleges in America. It was moved to Ashland, Virginia, in 1868.

Marker erected by the State of Virginia near the site of Randolph-Macon College at Boydton. The college was named for John Randolph and Nathaniel Macon, famous men of the period.

—Alpheus W. Potts

—from Simpson

Cokesbury Conference School, Cokesbury, South Carolina. It was founded in 1835 by the South Carolina Conference and named for Coke and Asbury. It was the successor of Mount Bethel Academy, Tabernacle Academy, and Mount Ariel Academy. Dr. Stephen Olin taught here.

—A. D. Betts

Cokesbury Conference School today

The Circuit Rider

AFTER the Revolution the amazing trek of the pioneers began moving westward. The Methodist preachers followed them on horseback. This was the era of the Circuit Rider, who rode the wilderness in search of souls as the hunter stalked his prey. They were the advance guard of civilization and morality, the most interesting, self-sacrificing breed of men known to American history, whose contributions are the legends of every American community.

Appalling dangers were braved daily by Methodism's "men on horseback," dangers from storms, swollen streams, wild beasts, Indians, desperadoes, hunger. They ate where and what they could; they slept in the woods when they could not find a cabin. How did they stand it? They didn't! They died! Of the first 650 preachers, 500 had to "locate." Of the first 737 who died, 203 were under thirty-five years old, and 121 were between thirty-five and forty-five. Nearly half died before they were thirty. Two thirds of those whose records are known died before they preached twelve years, and 199 died within the first five years.

The Circuit Rider

A church in the Virginia wilderness

A pioneer cabin in the forest

A frontier residence. The Circuit Riders had no churches as they swung their wide trail. Their pulpits were the cabins of the settlers, the taverns, brush arbors, the great out-of-doors. It was said that the first human sound in the wilderness was the ring of he frontiersman's ax; the second was the "hello" of the Circuit Rider who rode into his clearing. When storms were raging men remarked, "Nobody is out today except ducks and Circuit Riders!"

The arrival of the Circuit Rider

The Circuit Rider in action

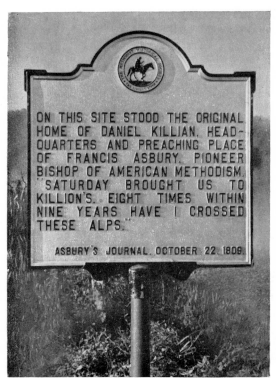

ON THIS SITE STOOD THE ORIGINAL HOME OF DANIEL KILLIAN. HEADQUARTERS AND PREACHING PLACE OF FRANCIS ASBURY, PIONEER BISHOP OF AMERICAN METHODISM. "SATURDAY BROUGHT US TO KILLION'S. EIGHT TIMES WITHIN NINE YEARS HAVE I CROSSED THESE ALPS."

ASBURY'S JOURNAL, OCTOBER 22, 1809.

Marker at the Killian House, one of Asbury's preaching places near Asheville, North Carolina, erected by the Methodist Historical Society

The Killian House, near Asheville, North Carolina, preaching place of Asbury

Marker erected by the Methodist Historical Society at the Shook House, Clyde, North Carolina, one of Asbury's preaching places. On November 30, 1810, he wrote in his *Journal:* "After crossing other streams, and losing ourselves in the woods, we came in, about nine o'clock at night, to Vater Shuch's. What an awful day!" More than sixty times Asbury crossed the Appalachian Mountains. One of his routes was the Cattaloochee Trail over the Great Smoky Mountains. Near its eastern end the Lake Junaluska Methodist Assembly is located.

—from Hurst

Slick Ford, Kentucky, Methodist Church, a typical meetinghouse on the frontier

The First Methodist Church in Kentucky, at Masterson
Station, near Lexington, where Asbury held a conference
in 1790. There were six members. Methodists crossed the
mountains and started the Holston Circuit in East Tennessee in 1783. The next year there was a Redstone Circuit
in Pennsylvania. Francis Clark, a settler and local preacher,
began preaching in Kentucky in 1783, the year after the
state was admitted to the Union. In 1786 Asbury sent James
Haw and Benjamin Ogden. The circuit was the whole state.
In 1787 there were 90 members; the next year there were
480; in 1796, 1,750, and Methodism was firmly established.

House near Masterson's Station in Kentucky where Asbury held the first Western Conference in 1790

New England

JESSE LEE, soldier of the Revolution and one of the notable leaders of early Methodism, was the founder of the church in New England, although he preached from Georgia to Maine. He was chaplain of the House of Representatives of the United States, author in 1810 of the first history of American Methodism, and in 1800 lacked but four votes of being elected to the episcopacy. In 1834 Cyrus Shephard went from the church at Lynn in company with Jason Lee to become a missionary teacher among the Flat Head Indians.

Benjamin Johnson house, Lynn, Massachusetts. Lee preached here in December, 1790. On February 20, 1791, he formed in Lynn the first Methodist church in the state, with eight members.

Town House at Fairfield, where Jesse Lee preached

The first Methodist Church at Lynn, Massachusetss, 1791.

Old St. David's Episcopal Church, Cheraw, South Carolina. While preaching here in 1785 Jesse Lee heard about the spiritual need of New England and resolved to go there.

—from Hurst

Jesse Lee preaching under "the old elm" on Boston Common, July 11, 1790. Richard Boardman had formed a small society in Boston in 1772, but it soon expired. Others preached in 1784 and earlier in 1790 but formed no societies.

First Methodist preaching house in Boston, 1795

Broomfield Street Church, Boston. The General Conference met here in 1852.

A conference group in Broomfield Street Church, Boston, 1833

—from Hurst

Readfield Meetinghouse, the first Methodist church in Maine, erected in 1795

Jesse Lee Memorial Church, East Readfield, Maine, 1795. Lee founded it, and Asbury held here the first Maine Conference.

Reverend Joshua Taylor, the first Methodist Presiding Elder in Maine, appointed in 1797

—from Hurst

Old Beech Hill Church, Granville, Massachusetts. In 1798 half of the New England Conference met here, the other half meeting in Maine.

The Camp Meeting Era

THE camp meeting swept the frontier at the beginning of the nineteenth century. Started by Presbyterians in Kentucky, it was taken over and practically monopolized by the Methodists. It met a great social need in the wilderness. Thousands of persons camped on the grounds, and evangelism was carried on from rude pulpits in brush arbors night and day by numerous preachers. The church grew rapidly as converts were numbered by the thousands in the most amazing religious phenomenon in American history. Extravagant emotional experiences, the "jerks," "barks," and similar exercises appeared. The camp meeting typed evangelism and experience in the area for a century.

Cane Ridge Church in Kentucky. Here in 1800 occurred the greatest and one of the earliest camp meeting revivals. It is now a church of the Disciples of Christ.

James Axley   Peter Cartwright

Cartwright and Axley were among the greatest of the camp meeting preachers. Cartwrights' *Autobiography* contains the best descriptions of the revivals. He worked in Logan County, Kentucky, which was called "Rogues Harbor" because an actual majority of the citizens were criminals in 1796.

—from an old print

A camp meeting

The First Camp Meeting Ground in Kentucky

Ohio

THE first Methodist sermon in Ohio was preached by George Callahan in 1787 at the request of settlers at Carpenter's Station. This was at the home of Regin Pumphrey in what is now Liberty County, West Virginia. John Kobler crossed the Ohio River from Kentucky in 1798 and from the home of Francis McCormick went on a tour through the valleys of the Miami and the Mad Rivers.

—from Barkley

The first Methodist church in Ohio and in the Northwest Territory, was erected in
1800 on Scioto circuit, Brush Creek, by Henry Smith

—from Hurst

The first Methodist church at Chillicothe,
Ohio, erected in 1807. Many notable Methodists were members of this church, among
them being Edward Tiffin, preacher, governor, and U.S. senator. His brother-in-law,
Thomas Worthington, attended Cokesbury
College and was governor and senator;
Judge Scott, a Methodist preacher, was
prominent in Ohio history.

—from Barkley

Francis McCormick entered Ohio from Kentucky around 1792 and formed at Millville the first Methodist circuit in Ohio and in the Northwest Territory, though Asbury had sent John Kobler to the region in 1789. When Asbury died in 1816, there were 18,150 Methodists in Ohio.

William Burke, Presiding Elder in the district which embraced Ohio. In 1811 he organized at Cincinnati the first Methodist station charge in Ohio.

—from Barkley

—from Hurst

The first Methodist church at Milford, Ohio, erected in 1816

—from Hurst

"Father" Wright's house near Edwardsville, Illinois, where
Bishop Roberts held the first conference in that state in 1817

—from Hurst

Bethel Meetinghouse, in the Old Goshen Settlement near Edwardsville, the first Methodist church in Illinois, built in 1805

AS early as 1801 the circuit riders reached Indiana from Kentucky and Ohio. Preaching places were established in Clark County, and William McKendree preached there in 1803. Camp meetings were held in 1806 or 1807, and in the latter year the Silver Creek circuit appeared on the minutes. Parts of the state were in the Ohio, Kentucky, and Missouri conferences. The Indiana conference was formed in 1832.

—from Sweet

First Methodist church in Indiana, three miles from Charleston, 1807-8

216

The first Methodist church in Michigan, erected about 1812

—from Hurst

Missouri

The Methodist Church at New Madrid, Missouri, the oldest operating society west of the Mississippi, founded in 1811

Old McKendree Chapel in Cape Girardeau County, near Jackson, Missouri, the oldest Methodist church west of the Mississippi River. It was built about 1806, and occasional services are still held in the building. Conferences were held here in 1819, 1821, 1826, and 1831 under Bishops George, Roberts, and Soule.

Texas

METHODIST preachers were early in Texas, but the first Methodist Society was formed by Henry Stephenson in 1833. Three missionaries were sent in 1837: Martin Ruter, Littleton Fowler, and Robert Alexander. Fowler became superintendent in 1838, and in 1842 he became financial agent and one of the founders of Rutersville College, now Southwestern University.

The first brick church in Texas

Littleton Fowler (1803-46)

Some Pioneers

S. R. Beggs, the first Methodist preacher appointed to Chicago

—from Luccock, Dixon, and Lee

J. B. Wakeley (1809-75), an outstanding preacher and author of New York and New Jersey. He wrote five books dealing with Methodist history.

Thomas Ware (1758-1842) attended the Christmas Conference and preached in Tennessee, North Carolina, Pennsylvania, and several other states. He was Book Agent, 1812-16.

William Winans (1788-1857). Born in Pennsylvania, he was a pioneer in Alabama, Mississippi, and Louisiana. He adhered to the Methodist Episcopal Church, South, in 1844.

The Death of Asbury

THE Prophet of the Long Road" died as he had lived, on the road. En route from Richmond, where he preached his last sermon, Bishop Asbury had to be carried into the home of George Arnold, where he died on March 31, 1816. In his last delirium the Bishop tried to take a collection for missions.

The home of George Arnold in Spottsylvania County, Virginia, where Bishop Asbury died

—J. Manning Potts

Marker at the site of the George Arnold house where Asbury died

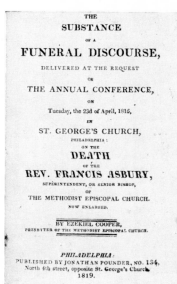

—from the author's collection

Title page of the funeral sermon of Bishop Asbury, preached by Ezekiel Cooper before the conference at St. George's Church in Philadelphia, April 23, 1816

Monument to Bishops Asbury, Emory, Waugh, and George in Mount Olivet Cemetery, Baltimore. Bishop Asbury was buried near the Arnold home in which he died. A month later his body was taken to Baltimore and placed under the pulpit of the Eutaw Street Church. Forty years later it was interred in the Mount Olivet Cemetery, Baltimore, where many early notables of Methodism sleep.

The Asbury Centennial Tablet, Baltimore

Road marker erected by the State of Virginia near the place where Asbury died

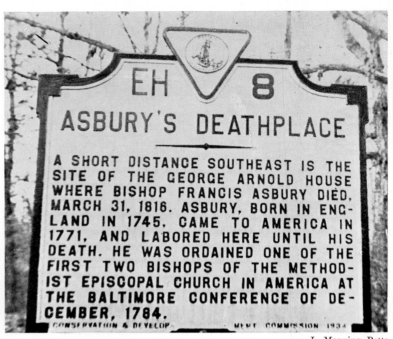

ASBURY'S DEATHPLACE

A SHORT DISTANCE SOUTHEAST IS THE SITE OF THE GEORGE ARNOLD HOUSE WHERE BISHOP FRANCIS ASBURY DIED, MARCH 31, 1816. ASBURY, BORN IN ENGLAND IN 1745, CAME TO AMERICA IN 1771, AND LABORED HERE UNTIL HIS DEATH. HE WAS ORDAINED ONE OF THE FIRST TWO BISHOPS OF THE METHODIST EPISCOPAL CHURCH IN AMERICA AT THE BALTIMORE CONFERENCE OF DECEMBER, 1784.

—J. Manning Potts

—J. Manning Potts

Plaque in Richmond where Asbury preached his last sermon on March 24, 1816. He was carried from his bed to the church, which stood on this spot, and was placed on a table to preach.

The Asbury Statue at Washington, D.C.

William McKendree

A VIRGINIAN and a soldier of the Revolution, McKendree was the real successor of Francis Asbury, with whom he traveled, both as a preacher and, more extensively, as a bishop. His outstanding service was rendered west of the Appalachian Mountains, and he was known as the Father of Western Methodism. His election to the episcopacy was attributed to a sermon which he preached at the General Conference of 1808. He is buried at Nashville, Tennessee.

—from an old print

Bishop McKendree entering an Indian village

Bishop William McKendree (1757-1835). Greatest of the early bishops after Asbury, McKendree was elected by the General Conference of 1808. He was the fourth bishop and the first native-born American in the office.

Strother's Meetinghouse, one of Mc-Kendree's preaching places near Nashville, Tennessee, now on the campus of Scarritt College

Some Early Bishops

Enoch George (1767-1828), fifth bishop of American Methodism, elected in 1816

Robert R. Roberts (1778-1843), the sixth bishop, elected in 1816, the first married man to occupy the office

Elijah Hedding (1780-1852), seventh bishop, elected in 1824

Beverly Waugh (1789-1858), eleventh bishop, elected in 1836

—from a painting in the State Capitol at Salem, Oregon

Jason Lee (1803-45), "Prophet of the New Oregon." He was appointed missionary to the Northwest in 1834. He was the founder of Salem, Oregon, and helped to secure the Northwest for the United States. Until he arrived in the Oregon country the gospel had never before been carried so far inland and under such difficulties. On Sunday, July 27, 1834, near the site of the future Fort Hall he preached the first Protestant sermon ever heard west of the Rocky Mountains.

The Circuit Rider of the Northwest. This statue stands on the grounds of the capitol of Oregon, at Salem. It was erected in honor of Reverend Robert Booth, one of the pioneer preachers of the Northwest.

The first mission in the Pacific Northwest, at Mission Bottom, about ten miles northwest of the present Salem, Oregon

Oregon Institute, founded at Salem, Oregon, by Jason Lee. It later became Willamette University

George Abernethy (1807-70), governor of Oregon, went as "missionary steward" with Jason Lee in 1839.

David E. Blaine, Methodist missionary, who built the First Methodist Church in Seattle in 1855

First Methodist Church, the pioneer church in Seattle, 1855

The Methodist church near Tacoma, Washington, built in 1854

J. H. Wilbur, who accompanied William D. Roberts to Oregon in 1847

Old Methodist church at Oregon City, Oregon, the first Protestant church west of the Rocky Mountains

Old Fort Nisqually, near Tacoma, near which Jason Lee established
his mission in 1834, as reconstructed

Whitman College, named in honor of Marcus Whitman, Northwest pioneer, who with Mrs. Whitman and other missionaries, was massacred by the Indians near Walla Walla, Washington, in 1847

—from Simpson

Willamette University, Salem, Oregon. Founded by Jason Lee in 1834 as the Oregon Mission Manual Labor School. In 1841 a new building was erected, and the name became the Indian Manual Training School. In the same school the Oregon Institute for Whites was opened in 1842. It became Willamette University in 1853.

—from Hurst

William Roberts. The Oregon and California Mission was authorized by the General Conference in 1848. William Roberts, who had arrived in Oregon in 1847, was the first superintendent. He organized the first Methodist church in San Francisco on his way to the Northwest.

California

WILLIAM ROBERTS formed the first Methodist church in San Francisco in 1847. But the real founders of Methodism in California were the missionaries who followed the forty-niners. Isaac Owen and William Taylor arrived in 1849. Jesse Boring, A. M. Wynn, and D. W. Pollock were appointed in the same year by the Methodist Episcopal Church, South, and they arrived in 1850.

William Taylor, Methodist missionary in California, India, South America, and Africa. One of the most spectacular figures of his generation, he traveled all over the world establishing "self-supporting" missions. He was elected missionary bishop for Africa in 1884.

Bishop O. P. Fitzgerald, Southern Methodist missionary in California, 1855 to 1878. He was superintendent of public instruction, and under his administration the University of California was established. He became a bishop of the Methodist Episcopal Church, South.

236

SHORTLY after the Civil War, Reverend J. J. Methvin began his long and notable missionary career among the Kiowas and other "wild tribes" or "blanket Indians." Among his converts were the Custer scouts, Kicking Bird, Hunting Horse, and Andele. The last was stolen in babyhood by raiding Indians and reared as a Kiowa. Recognized in young manhood and restored to his family, he could not endure the white man's life, and he returned to the Kiowas. He later became a Methodist preacher under the name of Andres Martinez.

Reverend J. J. Methvin, noted southern Methodist missionary among the wild tribes of Oklahoma

Andele, or Reverend Andres Martinez,
"the Kiowa captive"

—from Kansas Historical Collection

Shawnee Mission and First Labor School,
near Kansas City, 1830

James B. Finley (1781-1856), leader of Methodism in the Western Conference, and missionary to the Wyandot Indians

Old Fort Kearney, Nebraska City, 1847

Canada

VARIOUS bodies of American and British Methodists in Canada were united in 1884. In 1925 the United Church of Canada was formed, the Methodists taking into the union 4,107 churches, 418,352 members, 17 colleges, and 312 schools and social institutions. The United Church of Canada is a member of the World Methodist Council.

—from Hurst

William Black, the "Apostle of Novia Scotia," began preaching in Canada in 1779. He was instrumental in inducing the Christmas Conference to send preachers to Canada. In 1789 he was ordained by Bishops Coke and Asbury.

—from Hurst

Philander Smith, third bishop of the Methodist Episcopal Church of Canada, 1847-70

Enoch Wood, president of the Canada
Conference, 1851-58

St. James Methodist Church, Montreal, largest Protestant church in Canada

The Old Frame Meetinghouse, first
Methodist church in Toronto, 1818

The Old Hay Bay Church, first Methodist church in upper Canada. It was built in 1792, rebuilt in 1834, and used until 1864.

The Old Red Meetinghouse, Lundy's Lane, Canada, erected in 1817. The General Conference met here in 1820.

The first Methodist church in Montreal, 1807

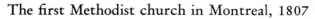

American Negro Methodism

THERE are 17,000 Negro Methodist churches and 2,000,000 members in the United States. The Central Jurisdiction of The Methodist Church has around 3,000 churches and 340,000 members. All the other Negro Methodists are in nine independent Negro denominations. These are:

Church	Members
African Methodist Episcopal Church	1,065,000
African Methodist Episcopal Zion Church	525,000
Colored Methodist Episcopal Church	385,000
African Union First Colored Methodist Protestant Church	2,500
Colored Methodist Protestant Church	200
Independent African Methodist Episcopal Church	1,500
Reformed Zion Union Apostolic Church	20,000
Reformed Methodist Union Episcopal Church	1,500
Union American Methodist Episcopal Church	10,000

Richard Allen, founder and first bishop of the African Methodist Episcopal Church. Negro members withdrew from a Methodist church in Philadelphia, and in 1799 Bishop Asbury ordained Richard Allen to serve them. In 1816 Allen led in the formation of the independent African Methodist Episcopal Church and became its first bishop. The African Methodist Episcopal Zion Church, formed in 1800, grew out of Zion Church in New York.

William Capers, founder of the Mission to the Slaves (1790-1885). In the South the Plantation Missions, under William Capers of South Carolina, sent white ministers to the slaves on the plantations and brought thousands of Negroes into the Methodist fold. In 1862, 327 plantation missionaries were at work, and the Methodist Episcopal Church, South, had 200,000 Negro members. These constituted one third of the total membership. Capers was elected a bishop by the first General Conference of the southern church in 1846.

—rare print from the author's collection

Bishop W. H. Miles, elected at the organizing General Conference of the Colored Methodist Church. In 1870 the General Conference of the Methodist Episcopal Church, South, at the request of its Negro members, authorized their formation into an independent church. Thus the Colored Methodist Episcopal Church was organized as a sister body of the southern church.

Bishop L. H. Holsey of the Colored Methodist Church

Dr. George Williams Walker of South Carolina, virtual creator of Paine College, Augusta, Georgia. In 1882 Paine College was established jointly by the Methodist Episcopal Church, South, and the Colored Methodist Episcopal Church, with interracial trustees and faculty. It was the pioneer co-operative institution of southern white people and southern Negroes.

Bishop Isaac Lane of the Colored Methodist Church

American Methodist Missions

AMERICAN Methodism is represented in fifty foreign lands, where it has around 5,000 churches and nearly 1,000,000 members, with many notable institutions. As in the case of British Methodism, which was carried abroad by emigrants from England, American Methodist missions resulted from the evangelistic passion of converts and not from deliberate administrative planning.

The beginnings constitute a romantic story of the interrelations of evangelism at home and the spread of the gospel "unto the uttermost parts of the world."

A converted drunk Negro, John Stewart, preached to the Indians in Ohio, and this led to the organization of the Methodist Missionary Society and the launching of missions in many lands.

The conversion of a German immigrant led to the spread of Methodism among the German-speaking people in America, the founding of the church in Germany, and the spreading from Germany of Methodism to Switzerland, Austria, Hungary, Yugoslavia, and other areas.

The conversion of Scandinavian seamen and immigrants on a Methodist mission ship in New York harbor resulted in widespread Scandinavian work in America and the beginnings of Methodism in the Scandinavian countries, Finland, the Baltic States, and Russia.

John Stewart and the
Organization of the Missionary Society

IN 1815 John Stewart, a Negro, was converted while drunk and started preaching to the Wyandot Indians in Ohio. In 1819 this mission was adopted by the Ohio Conference, and James Montgomery was appointed as a missionary. This was the beginning of actual missionary work. It led to the organization of the Methodist Missionary Society on April 5, 1819, in New York.

--from Hurst

The Old Wyandot Mission in 1886

—from Hurst

The Old Wyandot Mission as restored in 1889

Preaching to the Wyandots

German Methodism

BORN in 1807, William Nast came from Germany in 1828. Converted in 1835, he became a missionary to the Germans in Cincinnati, Ohio. Fifty years later there were 11 conferences, 761 churches, 63,260 members, 8 educational institutions, including 2 theological seminaries, 7 homes for children and the aged, a hospital, a publishing house, and periodicals among the German-speaking Methodists. This work was merged into the English-speaking conferences.

William Nast, father of organized German Methodism

Phillip Otterbein, a minister of the German Reformed Church, was a friend and associate of Asbury and assisted in Asbury's ordination. Asbury was not favorable to German-speaking societies, and Otterbein and others founded the United Brethren Church.

Henry Boehm (1775-1875), associate of Asbury, a Methodist preacher for three quarters of a century, preached the first sermon in German in Cincinnati. He was a leader of Methodism among the Germans.

Jacob Albright, German Methodist preacher and associate of Asbury and Henry Boehm, believed that his mission was to the Germans, and he became the founder of the Evangelical Church.

—from Hyde

Ludwig S. Jacoby, one of William Nast's converts, was the first American Methodist missionary to Germany, 1849.

The Methodist Book Concern and Tract House at Bremen, Germany, was destroyed in World War II, rebuilt at Frankfurt am Main.

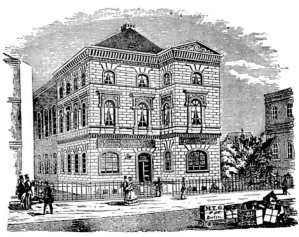

The Krameramthaus in Berlin, where the first Methodist sermon in Germany was preached, about 1850. There are today 5 Methodist conferences in Germany, with 400 churches, 225 ministers, and 60,000 members. Deaconess work began there; German Methodist deaconesses operate several fine hospitals and homes. There is a theological seminary at Frankfurt am Main. German Methodism is organized as a Central Conference and elects its own bishop.

—from Hurst

The Methodist Theological Seminary at Frankfurt am Main, Germany, founded about 1856. The first two German Methodist bishops were its principals.

—from Hurst

—from Hurst

Teuchelwald Rest Home and Conference Center for German Methodists at Freudenstadt in the Black Forest of Germany

—from Hurst

The Methodist Publishing House at Zurich, Switzerland, erected about 1890. Swiss Methodism was founded by German preachers, Ernst Mann and Hermann zur Jakobsmuhlen, in 1856. There are over 80 preachers and 15,000 members.

— from Hurst

Some Swiss Methodist Churches. *Top:*
Lenzburg; *center, left,* Berne; *right,*
Herisan. *Bottom:* Winterthur.

Scandinavian Methodism

IN 1845 the Methodists of New York fitted up a ship in the harbor as a mission for Scandinavian sailors and immigrants. It was called Bethelship, and on her decks hundreds were converted, among them the "Swedish Nightingale," Jenny Lind, the most famous singer of her day. Many Bethelship converts moved westward and developed whole conferences of Scandinavian Methodists in Michigan, Wisconsin, Illinois, and elsewhere. Others went back to their homeland and established Methodism in all the Scandinavian and Baltic countries.

The Bethelship "Henry Leeds," 1845

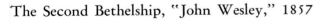

The Second Bethelship, "John Wesley," 1857

Ole Peter Petersen, Norwegian sailor and Bethelship convert, founder of Methodism in Norway, 1849

Olaf Gustaf Hedstrom, Swedish-born missionary on the Bethelship, 1845, and virtual founder of Scandinavian Methodism

Christian Willerup, a Dane and Bethelship convert, first superintendent of Methodism in Norway, 1856, and founder of Methodism in Denmark

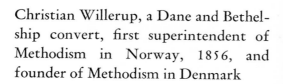

Norwegian-Danish Theological Seminary, Evanston, Illinois

—from Hurst

Jonas Hedstrom, Bethelship convert and founder of Methodism in Sweden. Men converted on the Bethelship established Methodism in Finland in 1866. Their Finnish converts carried it to Russia in 1889 and to what later became the Baltic States, Estonia, Latvia, and Lithuania, in 1904.

Swedish Theological Seminary, Evanston, Illinois

—from Hurst

The first Russian Methodist church, Wirballen, Russia, erected in 1909. In 1889 B. A. Carlson from Finland preached in Russia, and Heinrich Ramke, a Russo-German immigrant converted in America, went to Kovno in 1893. Russian Methodism was eliminated after the Bolshevik Revolution of 1917.

—from Hyde

—from Hurst

Rev. A. B. Carlson, one of the early leaders of Methodism in Finland, 1884

St. Paul's Methodist Church, Stockholm, Sweden. Methodism is represented in Norway (1856), Sweden (1850), Denmark (1858), Finland (1866), Lithuania (1904), Latvia (1912), and Estonia (1921). It is organized as the Central Conference of Northern Europe and elects its own bishop. There are about 30,000 members of the church in all these countries. Finland and the Baltic States have been practically detached since the ascendancy of Russia after World War II.

—from Hyde

Africa

THE first foreign missionary of American Methodism was sent to Liberia in 1833. He lived only four months after reaching Africa, and his dying words became a rallying cry of the period: "Let a thousand fall before Africa be given up."

Melville B. Cox, 1799-1833

—from Hurst

John Seys, successor to Melville Cox as Methodist missionary in Liberia

Bishop William Taylor, Methodist missionary pioneer on several continents, in native African dress

—from Hurst

Bishop Francis Burns, missionary in Liberia and first Negro bishop of the Methodist Episcopal Church. He was elected a missionary bishop by the Liberia Annual Conference in 1858, under the authorization of the General Conference of 1856.

"The Pathfinders," Bishop Walter R. Lambuth and Dr. John Wesley Gilbert, of the Colored Methodist Episcopal Church, founded the Mission of the Methodist Episcopal Church, South, at Wembo Nyama in the Belgian Congo in 1911.

THE Methodist Episcopal Church began missionary work in China in 1847. Judson D. Collins and Dr. Moses C. White were the first missionaries. Headquarters were at Foochow. Since they were not allowed to live within the walls, a residence and preaching place were established outside the old city.

Judson Dwight Collins, first Methodist missionary to China, 1847

Moses C. White, first Methodist missionary to China, 1847

The oldest Methodist church in China, Foochow

The first missionary residence outside Foochow

The first Methodist preachers ordained in China, Foochow, 1869

The first place of worship outside Foochow

William M. Wightman (1808-82). As editor of the *Southern Christian Advocate*, Charleston, South Carolina, William M. Wightman in 1845 wrote an editorial on "A Mission to China" which led his printer, Benjamin Jenkins, to volunteer as a missionary and was instrumental in founding the first foreign mission of the Methodist Episcopal Church, South, in 1846. Wightman was elected Bishop in 1866.

—from Hurst

above t ... se

money can be raised, you say, easily enough. It is only neccessary that a thing which so nearly concerns the obligations, self-respect, and character of Southern Methodism, should be brought forward. We will sustain it by acclamation. But there is a point you have overlooked in all this:—where will you find *a suitable man* for so delicate and difficult an enterprise as a mission to China?—He must be a man not too old, for a complicated and difficult language is to be mastered —not too young, for he represents a whole Church, and is charged with a commission which is to challenge respect from a community as wiley as the Chinese. He must have much of the fire and enthusiasm of youth, and yet this is to be

Extract from the Wightman editorial, 1845. Benjamin Jenkins, printer for the *Southern Christian Advocate*, Charleston, South Carolina, was led to volunteer as one of the first missionaries to China while setting the type for this editorial appeal.

Dr. Charles Taylor, first missionary of the Methodist Episcopal Church, South, to China, 1848. The first General Conference of the Methodist Episcopal Church, South, 1846, projected missionary work in China. Benjamin Jenkins and Dr. Charles Taylor were the first missionaries. They landed in 1848 and established the Southern Methodist Mission in the Shanghai area.

Miss Lochie Rankin, first missionary of the Woman's Missionary Society of the Methodist Episcopal Church, South, in China, 1878

—from Hyde

The first Annual Conference of the Methodist Episcopal Church, South, in China, 1876. The Americans are: *back row,* left to right: Dr. A. P. Parker, Dr. J. W. Lambuth, Dr. Young J. Allen, Dr. (later Bishop) Eugene R. Hendrix; *center:* Bishop Enoch M. Marvin. At this conference six Chinese preachers were ordained.

The Southern Methodists made the first convert (1851) and licensed the first preacher in China (1852). He was Lieu Sien-sang. On being baptized he took the name of James Andrew, after Bishop Andrew. They also built the first Methodist church in China, at Shanghai, in 1850.

Bishop Walter R. Lambuth. He served as a missionary in China and Japan and was a founder of Methodist missions in Manchuria, Africa, and Europe. He was a third generation missionary and the fifth generation of the Lambuth family are now on the field. He was Missionary Secretary and Bishop of the Methodist Episcopal Church, South.

Japan

AMERICAN Methodists first went to Japan in 1873. In 1907 the various Methodist bodies working there united to form the autonomous Japan Methodist Church. This merged, under government pressure, into the Church of Christ in Japan in 1840. There were then 500 Methodist churches and 30,000 members in the country. Methodism maintained seventeen of the finest institutions of learning, of all grades, in Japan. Outstanding were two great universities, Kwansei Gakuin, and Aoyama Gakuin and the famous Hiroshima Girls' School, destroyed by the atom bomb and later rebuilt.

Conference of the Methodist Episcopal Church, South, in Japan, 1900. *Center:* Bishop Alpheus W. Wilson.

Robert Samuel Maclay, founder
of Methodism in Japan, 1873

Korea

METHODISM entered Korea in 1884-85. In 1930 all branches of Methodism united to form the autonomous Korean Methodist Church, with Dr. J. S. Ryang as the first bishop. There was much confusion, destruction, and misunderstanding during World War II, and still more during the war between North Korea and South Korea which broke out in 1950. In normal times there were 900 Methodist churches with over 50,000 members in Korea.

The second General Conference of
the Korean Methodist Church, 1934

270

Baron Yun Chi Ho (T. H. Yun) of Korea, American-trained leader of Methodism in Korea.

India

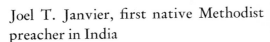

NDIA is the greatest foreign mission field of American Methodism. In India and Pakistan there are ten annual conferences, four bishops elected by the Central Conference, 800 Methodist churches, 327,000 members, 417,000 baptized children, eight colleges, four theological schools, nearly 600 village primary schools, and a dozen medical institutions.

Joel T. Janvier, first native Methodist preacher in India

—from Hurst

272

William Butler, founder and superintendent of the Methodist Mission in India, 1856

—from Hurst

Methodist missionary bishops in India. *Left to right*: Frank W. Warne, 1900; James M. Thoburn, 1888; Edwin W. Parker, 1900

—from Hurst

Founders of the Woman's Foreign Missionary Society of the
Methodist Episcopal Church, Boston, 1869. *Left to right*:
Mrs. Thomas Rich, Mrs. E. W. Parker, Mrs. Thomas Kings-
bury, Mrs. William Butler, Mrs. William Merrill, Mrs.
Lewis Flanders. In 1870 the Society sent to India its first
missionaries, Miss Isabella Thoburn and Dr. Clara Swain.

Nicholas Zamora, first native Methodist preacher in the Philippines, 1899

—from Hurst

—from Hurst

John Dempster, pioneer Methodist missionary in Argentina, 1836

Methodist Church in Buenos Aires

—from Hyde

—from Hurst

Reverend Francisco Penzotti, Methodist preacher and agent of the American Bible Society in Peru. Arrested and imprisoned at Callao for distributing the Bible in 1889, his case attracted world-wide attention.

274

Brazil

AFTER various attempts, beginning in 1835, Methodism was established in Brazil under Southern Methodist auspices in 1876. The first conference was organized in 1886, with three members. Reverend H. C. Tucker, Reverend James L. Kennedy, and Reverend John W. Tarbaux. In 1930 the autonomous Methodist Church of Brazil was set up. It has nearly 250 churches and 35,000 members, with a publishing house and fourteen institutions of learning.

—from Hurst

Southern Methodist Missionaries in Brazil, 1895

Reverend Daniel P. Kidder, early
Methodist missionary in Brazil, 1837

—from Hyde

—from Hurst

Justo Marcelino Euroza, first native
Methodist presiding elder in Mexico. The
autonomous Methodist Church of Mexico was formed in 1930 by a merger
of all American Methodist missionary
work. It has 140 churches and 21,000
members.

Czechoslovakia

DURING the Occupation of Czechoslovakia the Nazis blacked out all the objectionable songs in the Czech Methodist hymnbook. Methodism in Czechoslovakia started as relief work at the close of World War I. There are around 3,000 members. Since the Russian ascendancy following World War II, the work has been cut off from ecumenical Methodism and is practically independent.

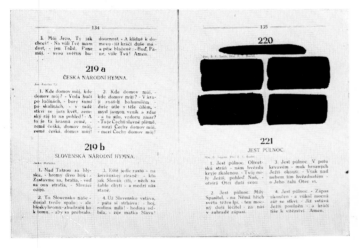

"My Country, 'Tis of Thee"

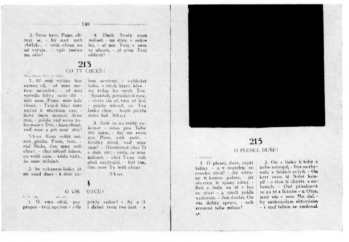

"Faith of Our Fathers"

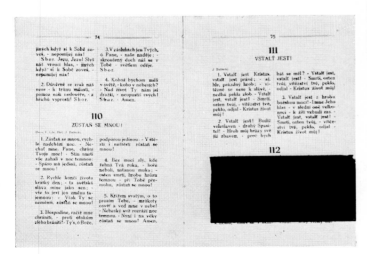

"Prayer for Our Country"

Poland

METHODISM entered Poland as a relief agency in 1920. The Methodist Mission was organized in 1922. Denied recognition and forbidden to use its own name, by 1939 it had only a dozen charges and a thousand members. After World War II recognition was granted, and there was remarkable growth. The government turned over scores of churches in the Silesia-East Prussia area, recovered from Germany, because the German pastors fled. In four years Methodism had fifty-five charges and a constituency of nearly 75,000. Polish Methodism is now detached from ecumenical Methodism and practically independent.

Methodist Church, Gierkowo, Poland

Methodist Church, Ostroda, Poland. This great church with a parish of a thousand souls was turned over to the Methodists after World War II.

The Bulgarian Mission, organized in 1892. Methodism was established in Bulgaria in 1857 by Wesley Prettyman and Albert L. Long. It was practically suppressed, and its superintendent, Yanko Ivanoff, was sentenced to life imprisonment in the Communist persecution of 1949.

—from Hyde

Methodist Summer Assembly, Stare Jablonki, Poland, formerly a rest home for German pastors.

—from Hurst

Leroy M. Vernon, founder of the Methodist Episcopal Church in Italy, 1871.

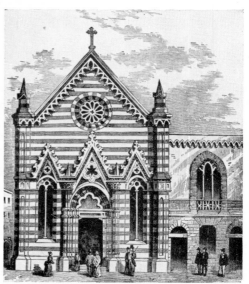

—from Hyde

St. Paul's Methodist Church in Rome, the first Protestant church in that city, 1875. Wesleyan Methodists established work in Italy in 1859. American Methodists entered in 1871. Scores of churches and several institutions were established. Under Fascist and Catholic persecution after 1929 all the institutions save one were closed. Italian Methodism became independent.

Methodist Publishing

FOLLOWING the example of John Wesley, who was one of the most prolific publishers of his time, American Methodism launched its own Publishing House in 1789 when John Dickins and Philip Cox were appointed "Book Stewards" and opened an office in Philadelphia in 1790. The first publications were "An Extract of the Christian's Pattern; or, A Treatise of the Imitation of Christ," by Thomas à Kempis, and the first volume of "The Arminian Magazine," both in 1789. Wesley's "Notes on the New Testament" followed. Other early books were the *Discipline*, "The Experience and Travels of Mr. Freeborn Garrettson," "A Pocket Hymn-Book," "An Extract on Infant Baptism," "Children's Instructions," and "An Abridgement of Mrs. Rower's Devout Exercises of the Heart."

—from Barker

Western Methodist Book Concern at Cincinnati, 1870-93

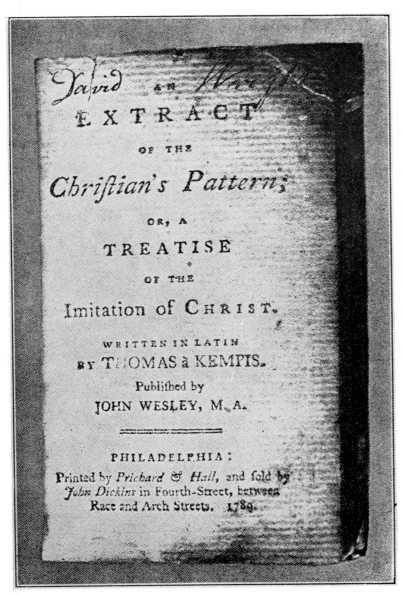

The first book published by the Methodist Church in America, 1789

Title page of the first number of "The Arminian Magazine," issued by John Dickins, publishing agent, in 1789

THE FOLLOWING

B O O K S,

ARE PUBLISHED BY

John Dickins,

No. 50, North Second-ſtreet, near Arch-ſtreet,
PHILADELPHIA;

*For the Uſe of the Methodiſt Societies in the
United States of America;*

AND THE PROFITS THEREOF APPLIED FOR THE
General Benefit of the ſaid Societies.

Sold by the Publiſher, and the Miniſters and Preachers
in the ſeveral Circuits.

———❊❀❊———

THE Rev. Mr. John Weſley's Notes on the
New Teſtament, in three volumes, well bound.
17s.——The ſame lettered, 18s. 6d.
The Arminian Magazine, vols. Iſt and IId, at 12s.
per volume.
Thomas à Kempis, bound, 2s.
The form of diſcipline for the Methodiſt Church,
as reviſed at the General Conference, 1792; with
Treatiſes on Predeſtination, Perſeverence, Chriſtian
Perfeſtion, Baptiſm, &c. all bound together, 4s. 3d.
The Experience and Travels of Mr. Freeborn Gar-
rettſon; well bound, 3s.
A Pocket Hymn-Book, containing three hundred
Hymns, well bound and lettered, 3s. 9d.
An Extraſt on Infant Baptiſm, ſtitched, 9d.
Children's Inſtruſtions, ſtitched, 6d.
An Abridgment of Mrs. Rowe's Devout Exerciſes of
the Heart, bound, 1s. 10½d.

*John Bankſon
1790*

THE
ARMINIAN MAGAZINE:

CONSISTING OF

EXTRACTS

AND

ORIGINAL TREATISES

ON

General Redemption.

VOLUME I.
For the YEAR 1789.

PRINTED IN PHILADELPHIA,
BY PRICHARD & HALL, IN MARKET STREET, AND SOLD BY
JOHN DICKINS, IN FOURTH STREET (EAST SIDE) NEAR
THE CORNER OF RACE STREET.
M.DCC.LXXXIX.

A page from the first catalogue of the Methodist Book Concern or Publishing House issued by John Dickins in 1795

The first number of *Zion's Herald*, issued January, 1823

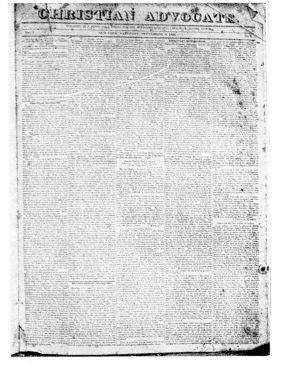

Title page of Jesse Lee's "Short History of the Methodists," 1810, the first history of American Methodism ever published

The first number of the *Christian Advocate*, issued September, 1826

Reverend Ezekiel Cooper succeeded John Dickins as book steward in 1798. The General Conference of 1808 adopted the Constitution which contained the "Restrictive Rules," one of which provides that the profits of the Book Concern or Publishing House must always be used for the superannuated preachers.

Nathan Bangs, book agent from 1820 to 1828. One of the outstanding men of his day, he was noted as a college president, editor, author, publishing agent, and missionary secretary.

—from Hurst

Headquarters of the Methodist Book Concern in New York, where it was located by the General Conference of 1804: (1) Old Wesleyan Academy Building, 1824-33; (2) 200 Mulberry Street, 1833-36 (destroyed by fire); (3) 200 Mulberry Street, 1836-69; (4) 805 Broadway, 1869-89; (5) 150 Fifth Avenue, 1888—.

AMERICAN Methodism has obeyed literally the command, "Go, teach." It sponsors more than 150 educational institutions in the United States and hundreds of all grades in its foreign fields. In America the church has nine universities, ten theological seminaries, sixty-nine colleges, twenty-four junior colleges, eight secondary schools, and thirty missionary institutions. They enroll a quarter of a million students, their properties and endowments are worth $420,000,000.

Augusta College, Augusta, Kentucky, 1823

—Tipple

Cornerstone of Bethel Academy, now a tablet in the Engineering Building at Vanderbilt University, Nashville, Tennessee. The first conference held in Kentucky in 1790 raised 300 pounds and established Bethel Academy. It opened near Lexington in 1794. In 1823 Augusta College was founded, the first of its grade since the burning of Cokesbury.

—from Simpson

Cazenovia Seminary, Cazenovia, New York. This institution was opened in 1824 as the Seminary of the Genesee Conference. The name was later changed to Oneida Conference Seminary and then to Cazenovia Seminary.

—from Simpson

Wesleyan University, Middletown, Connecticut. The oldest surviving educational institution related to American Methodism, Wesleyan began as an academy in 1825 and was chartered as a university in 1831.

—from Simpson

Wilbraham Academy, Wilbraham, Massachusetts, was established by Methodist ministers in 1818 at New Market, New Hampshire, and was moved to Wilbraham, Massachusetts, in 1825.

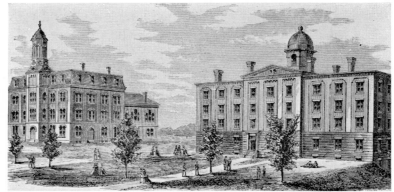

—from Simpson

Maine Wesleyan Seminary and Female College, Kent's Hill, Maine, was founded in 1821 at Readfield, Maine, as the Readfield Religious and Charitable Society and was later removed to Kent's Hill.

"Old West," the Administration Building at Dickinson College, Carlisle, Pennsylvania. Built in 1803 by Benjamin Latrobe, architect of the capitol at Washington, D. C., "Old West" is one of the oldest college buildings of American Methodism. Thomas Jefferson, James Madison, and Aaron Burr contributed funds for it, and President James Buchanan, who graduated from Dickinson in 1809, lived in "Old West" during his college career.

—from Simpson

—from Simpson

McKendree College, Lebanon, Illinois, was founded in 1828, with E. R. Ames, later bishop, as president. It was called Lebanon Seminary. In 1830 Bishop McKendree donated 480 acres of land and the name was changed.

Dickinson College, Carlisle, Pennsylvania, is the oldest Methodist college in America, although it has not been longest under Methodist control. Founded in 1783, it was taken over by the Philadelphia Conference in 1833. It was named for John Dickinson, Revolutionary patriot. Among its graduates were Chief Justice Taney and President Buchanan.

—from Simpson

—from Simpson

Williamsport Dickinson Seminary, Williamsport, Pennsylvania. Erected in 1812, it came under the patronage of the Baltimore Conference in 1848. In 1866 the name was changed and in 1869 it came under the control of the Central Pennsylvania Conference.

Allegheny College, Meadville, Pennsylvania, was chartered in 1817 and was under Presbyterian management until 1833. In that year the Pittsburgh Conference assumed control and Dr. Martin Ruter became president.

—from Simpson

—from Simpson

Syracuse University, Syracuse, New York. Genesee College was founded in 1849 at Lima, New York. In 1870 its patronage was transferred to Syracuse University, which was established in that year.

Wesleyan College, Macon, Georgia. Founded in 1836. It was the first college in America to confer a degree upon a woman.

Newbury Seminary and the Methodist Church, Newbury Vermont, 1833. The Seminary was moved to Montpelier in 1868 and became the Vermont Junior College in 1936.

—from Simpson

Troy Conference Academy Poultney, Vermont. This school was opened in a private house in 1836. In 1874 the Vermont Conference took over the institution.

Ohio Wesleyan University, Delaware, Ohio, founded in 1844

Original building of Indiana Asbury—De Pauw University, started in 1837, opened in 1840.

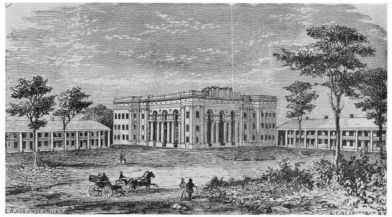

—from Simpson

Centenary College, Shreveport, Louisiana. Established at Jackson, by the state in 1825 as the College of Louisiana, it was taken over by the Methodist Episcopal Church, South, in 1845, and its name was changed. The college was moved to Shreveport in 1908.

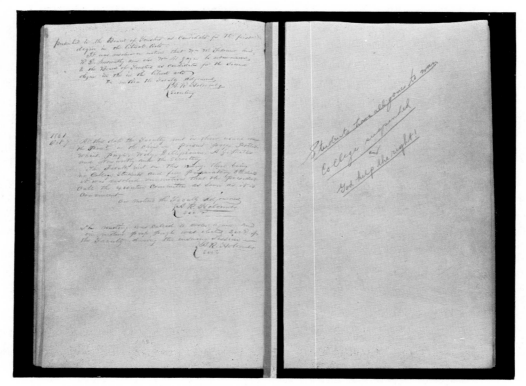

Minute Book of Centenary College, October 7, 1861. "Students have all gone to war. College suspended. God help the right!"

Braxton, Craven (1822-82) was president of Union Institute, later Trinity College, now Duke University in North Carolina, 1842-59.

James H. Carlisle was president of Wofford College, founded in 1854 at Spartanburg, South Carolina, by a gift from Benjamin Wofford, a local preacher.

Martin Ruter (1785-1838) was principal of the New Market Wesleyan Academy, 1818; founder of the Book Concern at Cincinnati, 1820; president of Augusta College in Kentucky, 1828; president of Allegheny College in Pennsylvania, 1834. He completed his career as superintendent of the mission in Texas.

293

Ignatius Few (1791-1845) was the founder and first president of Emory College, now Emory University, in Georgia.

Bishop Holland N. McTyeire (1824-89), was editor of the *New Orleans Christian Advocate*, 1854, and the *Nashville Christian Advocate*, 1858. Elected a bishop of the Methodist Episcopal Church, South, in 1866, he was instrumental in securing funds from the Vanderbilt family and founded and was the first Chancellor of Vanderbilt University, at Nashville, Tennessee, in 1875.

Stephen Olin (1797-1851) was principal of Tabernacle Academy, later the Cokesbury Conference School, in South Carolina, 1824; president of Randolph Macon College in Virginia, 1834; president of Wesleyan University in Connecticut, 1842.

Laban Clark (1778-1868) one of the founders and financial agent of Wesleyan University and one of the founders of the Missionary Society.

Wilbur Fisk, Principal of Wilbraham Academy in Massachusetts, 1825-31, and the first President of Wesleyan University in Connecticut, 1831.

Valentine Cook, Principal of Bethel Academy in Kentucky, 1799. He studied at Cokesbury College.

Peter Akers, President of McKendree College, Lebanon, Illinois, three times —1833, 1845, 1852.

MANY pioneer Methodists opposed special training for the ministry, and the *Discipline* of 1784 advised the preachers not to let their studies interfere with soul saving: "If you can do but one, let your studies alone." In 1841 theological training was started at the Newbury Academy in Vermont, and John Dempster, leading exponent of the idea, became the principal. The work was moved to Concord, New Hampshire, in 1846, and in 1876 it opened in Boston as the Boston Theological Seminary. It has been said that at least two thirds of the ministers were in opposition.

John Dempster, "Father of Theological Education in American Methodism"

Mrs. Eliza Garrett gave the funds for the founding of Garrett Biblical Institute at Evanston, Illinois. It opened in January, 1854, in a wooden building, with three teachers and four students. John Dempster was its principal.

Daniel Drew gave $600,000 to establish the Drew Theological Seminary, Madison, New Jersey. It opened in 1867. The president was the famous and scholarly Dr. John McClintock.

The Chapel at Duke University, Durham, North Carolina. Duke University and its Divinity School were heavily endowed by Mr. J. B. Duke. The University was formerly Trinity College, which dated from 1838.

—architect's model

Perkins School of Theology at Southern Methodist University, Dallas, Texas. Named for its greatest benefactors, Mr. and Mrs. J. J. Perkins, it has the finest physical plant of any Methodist theological seminary, dedicated in 1951.

Candler School of Theology at Emory University, Atlanta, Georgia, named in honor of Bishop W. A. Candler. Emory University was first founded at Oxford, Georgia, in 1836.

Boston University School of Theology, Boston, Massachusetts, 1876. Its history traces back to the Newbury Academy, Vermont, 1841.

Iliff University School of Theology,
Denver, Colorado, 1892

Thirkield Hall, Administration Building at Gammon Theological Seminary, Atlanta, Georgia

Mead Hall, Drew Theological Seminary, Madison, New Jersey, 1867

Westminster Theological Seminary, Westminster, Maryland. The Western Maryland College, founded in 1867, was one of the leading educational institutions of the Methodist Protestant Church.

The School of Religion at the University of Southern California, Los Angeles, California

Missionary Training

Fisk Hall, first building of the National College for Christian Workers, Kansas City, Missouri

Scarritt Bible and Training School, Kansas City, Missouri, founded by the woman's missionary organization of the Methodist Episcopal Church, South, in 1892 and named in honor of Nathan Scarritt, one of its benefactors

Scarritt College for Christian Workers, Nashville, Tennessee. Moved from Kansas City in 1924, it is the only institution of The Methodist Church that is owned by the General Conference.

Methodist Hospitals

THERE are seventy-five Methodist hospitals in the United States and a still larger number in foreign lands. Those in America serve 1,400,000 patients annually, and their properties and endowments are worth $65,000,000. The oldest is the Warren A. Candler Hospital at Savannah, Georgia, founded in 1830. The largest is Barnes Hospital at St. Louis, Missouri, with 847 beds. There are 178 homes for children and the aged under Methodist auspices in America, and these care for 10,000 persons and are worth $65,000,000.

Barnes Hospital,
St. Louis

Wesley Memorial Hospital,
Chicago

Some Early Methodist Hospitals. *Top:* Wesley Hospital, Chicago. *Center:* left, Seattle General Hospital; upper right, Christ's Hospital, Cincinnati; lower right, Sibley Memorial Hospital, Washington, D. C. *Bottom:* Asbury Hospital, Minneapolis.

Some Methodist Divisions

Lorenzo Dow (1777-1834)   Peggy Dow

Lorenzo Dow, an eccentric Methodist evangelist of the camp meeting era, was denied admission to the conferences but he preached widely. In 1810 he attempted to introduce the camp meeting in England, and his converts there formed the Primitive Methodist Church. His first wife, Peggy, was famous as his helper. Dow was buried in the Oak Hill Cemetery in Washington, D. C.

Hugh Bourne (1772-1852), one of Lorenzo Dow's followers in England, was expelled from the conference for "insufferable contumacy" when he persisted in holding camp meetings and was one of the founders of the Primitive Methodist Church. This church was organized in America in 1829, and Bourne emigrated in 1844.

307

William Clowes (1780-1851), one of the founders of the Primitive Methodist Church (or Connexion) in England in 1812

Orange Scott (1800-47). In 1840 a schism led by Orange Scott, Jotham Horton, L. R. Sunderland, L. C. Matlack, and others drew twenty-two preachers and 6,000 members out of the Methodist Espicopal Church. The dissidents opposed slaveholding in a paper called the *True Wesleyan*. They formed the Wesleyan Methodist Connection, which still survives.

The first Free Methodist Church, Clintonville, Illinois. In 1860 a group of holiness advocates, in protest against what they regarded as a decline in piety and the growth of worldly practices in the church, withdrew and formed the present Free Methodist Church.

IN 1830 a group left the Methodist Episcopal Church and formed the Methodist Protestant Church, because of their opposition to the episcopacy and the presiding eldership and their insistence on lay representation in the conferences. Their instrument was a publication called *The Mutual Rights*. The Methodist Protestant Church democratized its polity. It came into The Methodist Church in 1939.

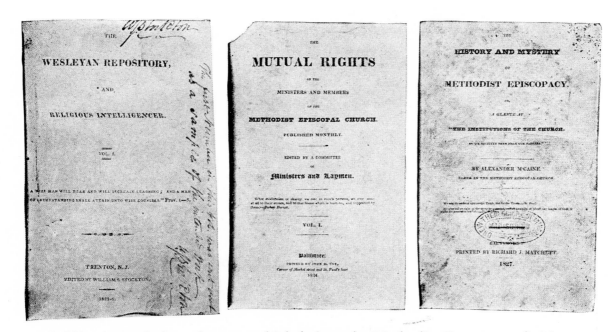

Publications of the reformers which led to the Methodist Protestant division.

—from Simpson

—from Simpson

George D. Brown (1792-1871). Author of the *Junius Letters*, addressed to the junior bishop, which opposed episcopacy and advocated lay representation in conferences, he was one of the leaders of the Reform Movement.

Nicholas Snethen (1769-1845). One of the leaders in the formation of the Methodist Protestant Church. He was a noted preacher and a traveling companion of Bishop Asbury.

—from Bassatt: History of the Methodist Protestant Church.

Three Leaders in the Formation of the Methodist Protestant Church. *Left to right:* D. B. Dorsey; J. S. Reese, M. D.; George D. Brown.

The Great Division

THE anti-slavery controversy became the occasion, if not the cause, of the division of American Methodism by the General Conference of 1844. Bishop Andrew, of Georgia, had inherited some slaves, and under the laws of Georgia he could not free them, though he offered to do so. The law of the church forbade the holding of slaves except in states which did not permit them to be liberated. The General Conference in 1844 adopted a resolution requesting Bishop Andrew to cease exercising his episcopal functions so long as "the impedient remains."

The Southern delegates took the ground that Bishop Andrew had been deposed without a trial and without violating any law of the church, the action made impossible Methodist work in the South and among the slaves, and the General Conference passed on the constitutionality of its own action. The Northern delegates contended that to permit a slaveholder to exercise the functions of a bishop would be an endorsement of slavery. Sentiment in many Northern conferences made it impossible for a slaveholding bishop to preside.

Bishop James O. Andrew (1794-1871)

311

The Plan of Separation

THE General Conference adopted the famous Plan of Separation. It provided that:
"All the societies, stations, and Conferences adhering to the Church in the South, by a vote of the majority of said societies, stations, and Conferences, shall remain under the unmolested pastoral care of the Southern Church; and the ministers of the Methodist Episcopal Church shall in no wise attempt . . . to exercise any pastoral oversight therein; it being understood that the ministry of the South reciprocally observe the same rule in relation to stations, societies, and Conferences adhering by vote of a majority, to the Methodist Episcopal Church; provided also, that this rule shall apply only to societies, stations, and Conferences bordering on the line of division, and not to interior charges, which shall in all cases be left to the care of that church within whose territory they are situated."

The Plan also provided for the equitable division of Book Concern property and all superannuate and other general funds.

Fourth Street Methodist Church, Louisville, Kentucky. Acting under the Plan of Separation, the Southern Conferences elected delegates to a Convention, which met in Fourth Street Church and decided to organize the Methodist Episcopal Church, South.

—from Arnold

312

Green Street Methodist Church, New York, where the General Conference of 1844 was held

Methodist Episcopal Church, South

THE first General Conference of the Methodist Episcopal Church, South, met in Petersburg, Virginia, in May, 1846. Its business sessions were held in a Negro church, for the Union Street Church was turned over to its Negro members in 1842. The new church retained the same law on slavery which existed in the Methodist Episcopal Church.

Union Street Church, Petersburg, Virginia, 1818-42

Bishop Joshua Soule (1781-1867) was the greatest episcopal leader of early Methodism after Asbury and McKendree. He was the author of the plan for a delegated General Conference and wrote the constitution of the church when he was thirty-one years of age. He was book agent, 1812-16, and founder and editor of the *Methodist Magazine*. In 1820 he was elected to the episcopacy, but he refused the office because of his belief that the General Conference had violated the constitution, which he had prepared, by providing for the election, rather than the appointment, of presiding elders. This act having been rescinded, he accepted his second election in 1824. Though born in Maine and having spent his previous ministerial career in the North, he adhered to the Methodist Episcopal Church, South, in 1844.

JOHN PHILIP NEWMAN TRUSTEN POLK CLINTON B. FISK

DAVID CLOPTON REV. M. D'C. CRAWFORD

JUDGE ENOCH FANCHER EDWARD HOWELL MYERS ROBERT KENNON HARGROVE

Some members of the Cape May Commission. After 1844 a change of sentiment occurred in the North. The Northern Annual Conferences voted against changing the Restrictive Rule to permit the division of the Book Concern and funds as provided in the Plan of Separation. The Plan of Separation was, however, upheld by the United States Supreme Court. In 1876 the Cape May Commission appointed by the two churches unanimously declared that both were legitimate branches of Episcopal Methodism organized in 1784.

Publishing Houses of the Methodist Episcopal Church, South, Nashville, Tennessee (*Top*, 1854; *bottom*, 1872).

—from Hurst

Some Methodist Bishops. D. S. Doggett, 1866; William M. Wightman, 1866; George F. Pierce, 1854; Beverly Waugh, 1836; John Emory, 1832. Doggett, Wightman, and Pierce were Bishops of the Methodist Episcopal Church, South. Emory and Waugh were elected before the division of the church in 1844.

Some Bishops of the Methodist Episcopal Church. Thomas A. Morris, 1836; Edmund S. Janes, 1844; Matthew Simpson, 1852; Levi Scott, 1852; Osmond C. Baker, 1852; Edward Thomson, 1864; Edward R. Ames, 1852; Davis W. Clark, 1864; Calvin Kingsley, 1864.

ROBERT PAINE

LOVICK PIERCE

H. B. BASCOM

JOHN EARLY

H. H. KAVANAUGH

Some Southern Methodist Leaders. Bishop Robert Paine, 1846; Bishop Henry B. Bascom, 1850; Dr. Lovick Pierce, father of Bishop George F. Pierce; Bishop John Early, 1854; Bishop H. H. Kavanaugh, 1854.

Some Southern Methodist Bishops. R. K. Hargrove, 1882; Linus Parker, 1882; John C. Keener, 1870; John C. Granbery, 1882; Alpheus W. Wilson, 1882.

J. B. McFERRIN

ROBT ALEXANDER

W.G.E. CUNNYNGHAM

SAMUEL CHICOTE
CHIEF OF MUSKCOEES

O. P. FITZGERALD

THOS O. SUMMERS

Some Southern Methodist Leaders. *Left to right, top:* Robert Alexander, J. B. McFerrin, missionary to the Indians, editor of the *Southwestern Christian Advocate* (1840), book agent (1858), missionary secretary (1866); W. G. E. Cunnyngham. *Bottom:* Bishop O. P. Fitzgerald, Samuel Chicote, Indian chief and missionary to the Indians, Thomas O. Summers, missionary in Texas (1840), editor of *Southern Christian Advocate* (1846), book editor and editor of *The Quarterly Review* and *Christian Advocate* at Nashville (1855), professor of Systematic Theology and dean of the Theological Faculty at Vanderbilt University.

Unification

EFFORTS to reunite the branches of American Methodists were crowned with success in 1939, when the Methodist Episcopal Church, the Methodist Episcopal Church, South, and the Methodist Protestant Church united to form The Methodist Church, the largest Protestant body in the United States.

Bishop Earl Cranston, *left,* of the Methodist Episcopal Church, and Bishop Eugene R. Hendrix of the Methodist Episcopal Church, South, advocates of Methodist unification, at the Northern General Conference in 1916.

The Bishops of the Methodist Episcopal Church and the Methodist Episcopal Church, South, with leaders of the Methodist Protestant Church at the time of the Unification of American Methodism.

Ordination of J. C. Broomfield, of the Methodist Protestant Church, as a bishop of The Methodist Church at the Uniting Conference, Kansas City, Missouri, 1939. The Methodist Protestant Church was not episcopal in nature, and its delegates at the Uniting Conference elected Bishops J. C. Broomfield and James H. Straughn.

Methodist Unification Proclaimed

Left to right: Bishop James H. Straughn of the Methodist Protestant Church, Bishop Edwin Holt Hughes of the Methodist Episcopal Church, and Bishop John M. Moore of the Methodist Episcopal Church, South, clasp hands on the stage at the Uniting Conference, 1939.

Bishops of American Episcopal Methodism

—arranged by Dorothy Magee

Bishops of the Methodist Episcopal Church prior to the Division of Methodism in 1844

—arranged by Dorothy Magee

Bishops of the Methodist Episcopal Church after 1844

JAMES M. THOBURN
1888
missionary bishop

JAMES N. FITZ GERALD
1888

ISAAC W. JOYCE
1888

JOHN P. NEWMAN
1888

DANIEL A. GOODSELL
1888

JOSEPH C. HARTZELL
1896
missionary bishop

CHARLES C. McCABE
1896

EARL CRANSTON
1896

DAVID H. MOORE
1900

JOHN W. HAMILTON
1900

EDWIN W. PARKER
1900
missionary bishop

JOSEPH F. BERRY
1904

HENRY SPELLMEYER
1904

WILLIAM F. McDOWELL
1904

JAMES W. BASHFORD
1904

WILLIAM BURT
1904

LUTHER B. WILSON
1904

THOMAS B. NEELY
1904

JOHN E. ROBINSON
1904
missionary bishop

ISAIAH B. SCOTT
1904
missionary bishop

MERRIMAN C. HARRIS
1904
missionary bishop

WILLIAM F. ANDERSON
1908

JOHN L. NUELSEN
1908

WILLIAM A. QUAYLE
1908

CHARLES W. SMITH
1908

WILSON S. LEWIS
1908

EDWIN H. HUGHES
1908

ROBERT McINTYRE
1908

FRANK M. BRISTOL
1908

HOMER C. STUNTZ
1912

THEODORE S. HENDERSON
1912

WILLIAM O. SHEPARD
1912

NAPHTALI LUCCOCK
1912

FRANCIS J. McCONNELL
1912

FREDERICK D. LEETE
1912

RICHARD J. COOKE
1912

WILBUR P. THIRKIELD
1912

WILLIAM P. EVELAND
1912
missionary bishop

HERBERT WELCH
1916

THOMAS NICHOLSON
1916

ADNA W. LEONARD
1916

MATTHEW S. HUGHES
1916

—arranged by Dorothy Magee

Bishops of the Methodist Episcopal Church after 1844

326

—arranged by Dorothy Magee

Bishops of the Methodist Episcopal Church after 1844

WILLIAM CAPERS 1846 ROBERT PAINE 1846 HENRY B. BASCOM 1850 GEORGE F. PIERCE 1854 JOHN EARLY 1854 H. H. KAVANAUGH 1854

WILLIAM M. WIGHTMAN 1866 ENOCH M. MARVIN 1866 DAVID S. DOGGETT 1866 H. N. MCTYEIRE 1866 JOHN C. KEENER 1870 A. W. WILSON 1882 LINUS PARKER 1882

JOHN C. GRANBERY 1882 ROBERT K. HARGROVE 1882 WILLIAM W. DUNCAN 1886 CHARLES B. GALLOWAY 1886 EUGENE R. HENDRIX 1886 JOSEPH S. KEY 1886 ATTICUS G. HAYWOOD 1890

O. P. FITZGERALD 1890 H. C. MORRISON 1898 ELIJAH E. HOSS 1902 ALEX. C. SMITH 1902 J. J. TIGERT 1906 SETH WARD 1906 JAMES ATKINS 1906 JOHN C. KILGO 1910

WM. B. MURRAH 1910 WALTER R. LAMBUTH 1910 R. G. WATERHOUSE 1910 EDWIN D. MOUZON 1910 JAMES H. MCCOY 1910 WM. F. MCMURRY 1918 WM. B. BEAUCHAMP 1922 JAS. E. DICKEY 1922

—arranged by Dorothy Magee

Bishops of the Methodist Episcopal Church, South

Bishops of the Methodist Episcopal Church, South, at the time of Unification, 1939

Bishops of The Methodist Church, 1939-48

The Big Ten

THE statistical office of The Methodist Church has published a list of the ten largest churches of American Methodism. Seven of the ten are in the South, and four of these are in Texas; two are in the Central Jurisdiction; one is in Michigan.

First Methodist Church, Houston, Texas, the largest church in American Methodism, 8,070 members (1951).

Metropolitan Methodist Church, Detroit, Michigan, 6,553 members (1951).

329

330

First Methodist Church, Dallas, Texas, 4,961 members (1951).

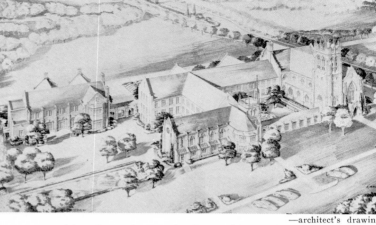

—architect's drawing

Highland Park Methodist Church, Dallas, Texas, 6,160 members (1951).

First Methodist Church, Birmingham, Alabama, 4,310 members (1951).

Travis Park Methodist Church, San Antonio, Texas, 5,225 members (1951).

St. Luke's Methodist Church, Oklahoma City, Oklahoma, 4,837 members (1951).

—architect's drawing

First Methodist Church, Shreveport, Louisiana, 5,202 members (1951).

Tindle Temple Methodist Church, Philadelphia, Pennsylvania, 5,957 members (1951).

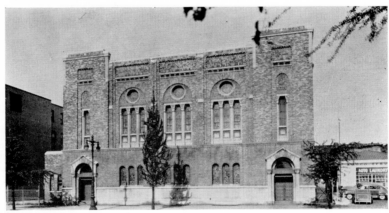

St. Mark's Methodist Church, Chicago, Illinois, 4,580 members (1951).

The Council of Bishops

The Council of Bishops of The Methodist Church at the Grand Canyon, 1951

The Methodists of the World

Approximate membership statistics, including preparatory members.

EUROPE

British Isles	Membership
Methodist Church in Great Britain	750,600
Methodist Church in Ireland	31,800
Wesleyan Reform Union	6,100
Independent Methodist Churches	7,700

Continental Europe

(The Methodist Church, U.S.A., except in France, Italy and Portugal)

Austria	2,000
Belgium	1,100
Bulgaria	2,400
Czechoslovakia	3,000
Denmark	3,500
Estonia, Latvia, Lithuania	3,000
Finland	3,000
France	1,700
Germany	60,500
Hungary	700
Italy	5,000
Norway	9,000
Poland	10,000
Portugal	500
Spain	400
Sweden	11,500
Switzerland	11,900
Yugoslavia	3,000
Total in Europe	928,400

NORTH AMERICA

United States of America

The Methodist Church	9,066,000
Apostolic Methodist Church	100
Congregational Methodist Church	11,000
Congregational Methodist Church of U.S.A., Inc.	6,000
Evangelical Methodist Church	5,000
Free Methodist Church	50,000
Holiness Methodist Church	1,000
New Congregational Methodist Church	1,500
Primitive Methodist Church	12,000
Reformed Methodist Church	500
Reformed New Congregational Methodist Church	500
Wesleyan Methodist Church of America	33,000
Southern Methodist Church	6,000
African Methodist Episcopal Church	1,066,000
African Methodist Episcopal Zion Church	525,000
African Union First Colored Methodist Protestant Church	2,500
Colored Methodist Episcopal Church	385,000
Colored Methodist Protestant Church	200
Independent African Methodist Episcopal Church	1,500
Reformed Zion Union Apostolic Church	20,000
Reformed Methodist Union Episcopal Church	1,500
Union American Methodist Episcopal Church	10,000
Total in U.S.A.	11,204,300

Canada

United Church of Canada (Approximately two-thirds of 792,000 members.)	528,000

Mexico

Methodist Church of Mexico	15,600
Free Methodist Church	700
Totals for North America	11,748,600

CENTRAL AND SOUTH AMERICA

Guatemala

Primitive Methodist Church	600

Honduras

Methodist Church in U.K.	500

British Honduras

Methodist Church in U.K.	1,100

334

Costa Rica
Methodist Church in U.K. 300
Methodist Church in U.S.A. 300

Panama Republic and Canal Zone
Methodist Church in U.K. 1,600
Methodist Church in U.S.A. 200
Free Methodist Church 100

Colombia
Wesleyan Methodist Church of U.S.A.... 100

British Guiana
Methodist Church in U.K. 5,300
African Methodist Episcopal Church..... 200
African Methodist Episcopal Zion Church 600

Dutch Guiana
Methodist Church in U.K. 100
African Methodist Episcopal Church 200

Peru
Methodist Church in U.S.A. 500

Bolivia
Methodist Church in U.S.A. 300

Brazil
Methodist Church of Brazil 33,400
Free Methodist Church 100

Chile
Methodist Church in U.S.A. 6,000
Methodist Pentecostal and Evangelical
Pentecostal, offshoots from Methodism
with a Methodist background........ 130,000

Argentina
Methodist Church in U.S.A. 5,400

Paraguay
Free Methodist Church 500

Uruguay
Methodist Church in U.S.A. 1,000

Total, S. and Cen. America.......... 188,400

WEST INDIES

Bahamas
Methodist Church in U.K. 2,700
African Methodist Episcopal Church..... 100

Cuba
Methodist Church in U.S.A. 6,000

Jamaica
Methodist Church in U.K. 18,800
African Methodist Episcopal Church..... 500

Haiti
Methodist Church in U.K. 1,700
African Methodist Episcopal Church..... 100

Dominican Republic
African Methodist Episcopal Church..... 500
Free Methodist Church 1,200
Methodist Church (Union) 1,000

Puerto Rico
Methodist Church in U.S.A............ 3,800

Virgin Isles
Methodist Church in U.K. 1,700
African Methodist Episcopal Church..... 900
African Methodist Episcopal Zion Church 400

Lesser Antilles (British, including Barbados)
Methodist Church in U.K. 20,200
African Methodist Episcopal Church..... 300

Lesser Antilles (Dutch, chiefly Curacao)
Methodist Church in U.K. 1,200

Trinidad and Tobago
Methodist Church in U.K. 3,700
African Methodist Episcopal Church..... 400
United Church of Canada 1,600

Total in West Indies 66,800

ASIA

Japan
Church of Christ in Japan (a united church
of 133,000 members; the last figures for
the communicant membership of the Japan Methodist Church are given) 44,800
Free Methodist Church 2,000
Wesleyan Methodist Church of U.S.A.... 600

Okinawa
Methodist Church (Union) 100

Korea
Korean Methodist Church 43,100

Manchuria
Korean Methodist Church 1,500

China

Methodist Church in U.K.	41,200
Methodist Church in U.S.A.	58,800
Free Methodist Church	700
Wesleyan Methodist Church of U.S.A.	100
United Church of Canada (two-thirds)	3,300

Malaya

Methodist Church in U.S.A.	9,100

British Borneo (Sarawak)

Methodist Church in U.S.A.	3,000

Philippine Islands

Methodist Church in U.S.A.	63,300
Evangelical Methodist Church of the Philippines	20,000

Sumatra

Methodist Church in U.S.A.	4,000

India and Pakistan

Church of South India. (Into this church of 244,600 members went from the Methodist Church in U.K.)	144,000
Methodist Church in U.S.A.	327,000
(Full members 101,000; preparatory members 226,000; baptized children 417,000.)	
Methodist Church in North India (Australasian)	3,500
Methodist Church in U.K. (North India)	4,200
Free Methodist Church	300
Wesleyan Methodist Church of U.S.A.	100
United Church of Canada (two-thirds)	14,600

Burma

Methodist Church in U.K.	900
Methodist Church in U.S.A.	900

Ceylon

Methodist Church in U.K.	10,000
Total in Asia	801,100

AFRICA

Algeria and Tunisia

Methodist Church in U.S.A.	300

Ivory Coast

Methodist Church in U.K.	20,500

Dahomey and French Togoland

Methodist Church in U.K.	7,500

Fernando Po

Methodist Church in U.K.	3,400

Madeira Islands

Methodist Church in U.S.A.	500

Gambia

Methodist Church in U.K.	1,100

Sierra Leone

Methodist Church in U.K.	8,100
West African Methodist Church	2,000
African Methodist Episcopal Church	300
Wesleyan Methodist Church of U.S.A.	500

Liberia

Methodist Church in U.S.A.	22,000
African Methodist Episcopal Church	1,200
African Methodist Episcopal Zion Church	2,300

Gold Coast

Methodist Church in U.K.	50,600
African Methodist Episcopal Church	800
African Methodist Episcopal Zion Church	4,000

Nigeria

Methodist Church in U.K.	52,800
African Methodist Episcopal Church	30,000
African Methodist Episcopal Zion Church	2,500

Belgian Congo

Methodist Church in U.S.A.	33,000
Free Methodist Church	2,800

Angola

Methodist Church in U.S.A.	19,000
United Church of Canada (two-thirds)	3,300
Wesleyan Reform Union	100

South Africa

Methodist Church of South Africa	227,600
Methodist Church in U.S.A.	800
African Methodist Episcopal Church	35,000
Free Methodist Church	1,200
(The 1936 South African census returned 1,019,616 Methodists.)	

Southern Rhodesia

Methodist Church in U.K.	17,900
Methodist Church in U.S.A.	25,000
Free Methodist Church	400

Northern Rhodesia

Methodist Church in U.K. 1,700

Mozambique (Portuguese East Africa)

Methodist Church in U.S.A. 5,000
Free Methodist Church 2,400
Methodist Church of South Africa 900

Kenya

Methodist Church in U.K. 2,700

Total in Africa 589,200

AUSTRALASIA

Australia

Methodist Church of Australasia 206,500
(Census reports 683,000 Methodists)

New Zealand

Methodist Church of New Zealand 35,300
(Census reports 130,000 Methodists)

Indonesia

Methodist Church in U.S.A. 3,500

Melanesia (New Guinea, Papua)

Methodist Churches of Australia and N.Z. 10,300

Solomon Islands

Methodist Church of N.Z. 9,900

Fiji Islands

Methodist Church of Australia 31,700

Samoa

Methodist Church of Australia 4,300

Tonga

Methodist Church of Australia 4,900

Hawaiian Islands

Methodist Church in U.S.A. 3,900

Total in Australasia 310,300

TOTALS

EUROPE

British Isles 796,200
Continental Europe 132,200

AMERICA

United States of America 11,204,300
Canada 528,000
Mexico 16,300
Central and South America 188,400
West Indies 66,800

AFRICA 589,250

ASIA 568,500

AUSTRALASIA 310,300

Grand Total, World Methodism 14,400,250